"You won't believe this, but . . ."

Responding to Student Complaints and Excuses

Gary Colwell

Detselig Enterprises Ltd.
Calgary, Alberta

© 1996 **Gary Colwell**

Concordia University College of Alberta
Edmonton, Alberta

Canadian Cataloguing in Publication

Colwell, Gary, 1944-

You won't believe this, but —

ISBN 1-55059-137-1

1. Teacher-student relationships. 2. Interaction analysis in
    education. 33. School discipline. I. Title.
LB1033.C65 1996   371.1'023   C96-910084-1

Detselig Enterprises Ltd.
1220 Kensington Road NW
Calgary, Alberta T2N 3P5

Distributed by:

Temeron Books Inc.
1220 Kensington Road NW
Calgary, Alberta T2N 3P5

Temeron Books Inc.
P.O. Box 896
Bellingham, WA 98227

Printed in Canada   SAN 115-0324   ISBN 1-55059-137-1

To Sheila

Detselig Enterprises Ltd. appreciates the financial assistance for its 1996 publishing program from the Department of Canadian Heritage and the Alberta Foundation for the Arts, a beneficiary of the Lottery Fund of the Government of Alberta.

COMMITTED
TO THE
DEVELOPMENT
OF CULTURE
AND
THE ARTS

ALBERTA
Lotteries

The Alberta
Foundation
for the Arts

Alberta

Preface

There is nothing that testifies so eloquently to the power of human creativity as our complaints and excuses. Being acutely adept at finding weaknesses in other people, we are also infinitely inventive at making excuses for ourselves. Sometimes our complaints *do* reflect the inadequacies of the world outside us, but just as often they reflect the inadequacies of the world within: our conceptions, our reasoning, our moral training, and our attitudes. This propensity to locate the source of our faults, and the personal dissatisfaction which derives from them, in the world beyond our control, is something that afflicts all of us, including students.

As a university college instructor I have noticed that a large number of student complaints and excuses recur. Year after year the faces change, but most of the complaints and excuses remain essentially the same. Because their nature, origin and frequency have been of interest to me for some time, I have decided to discuss them in this collection of fifteen case studies. If the people whose lives are adversely affected by them are helped in some small way, I shall be amply rewarded.

Students who are willing to look at themselves through the eyes of one who teaches them may be saved from making complaints and excuses which their instructors will not likely find convincing. Indeed, such complaints and excuses will likely create suspicion in their instructors. Then, too, the discussions can serve as authentic case material for instructors who teach courses in informal logic, for many types of informal fallacies have been identified. I also believe that colleagues who teach in a wide variety of academic disciplines will derive some benefit from these discussions. Perhaps they will take some satisfaction from knowing that they are not alone in receiving perennial complaints and that some effective responses are ready at hand, should such ever be needed or wanted.

People outside academia, especially those in the helping professions, must also contend with complaints. Some of the complaints discussed here are like those heard by teachers and social workers, therapists and clergypersons, and people on both sides of the business counter in companies too numerous to mention. The widespread nature of such complaints reflects not only a failure in reasoning but a failure in moral training as well.

Since every case in the book comes from my teaching experience and the discussions of them originate from the perspective of one philosophy instructor, this work is not a sociological study. I have discovered, however, that most of these cases are ones with which many of my fellow instructors have had to deal, and their disciplines cover a wide range of subject matter, from English to mathematics.

This may mean of course that the responses which I have given are not the ones which other instructors would give in the same circumstances. And their responses might be better than mine. So, I invite all readers to examine my arguments and improve upon them where they can, and if anyone feels inclined to write to me about the error of my ways I shall be pleased to hear from him or her. Since my study is not exhaustive I should also like to hear about chronic complaints not included here.

I deal with the complaints and excuses in a fairly straightforward manner. In the first three sections I simply follow the academic calendar. Beginning with a student complaint on the first day of classes, I then proceed to discuss some excuses and complaints which arise later in the term, ones about late essays and about essays which receive poor grades. Then follows a discussion of some common complaints which are made about the results of tests, exams and classmarks. While some of the complaints in Chapters 1 to 3 might be classified as partially irrelevant complaints, the complaints in Chapter 4 are even more irrelevant to the requests they are used to support; hence the ambiguous title of Chapter 4: "More Irrelevant Complaints." Occasionally a complaint can be downright nasty and disruptive, and it is with this type of complaint that I deal in Chapter 5. All student complaints must begin and end, I suppose, with the alleged shortcomings of the instructor. Chapter 6 examines some of the complaints which students make about what they perceive to be the wrong expectations and attitudes of their instructor. In Chapter 7 I acknowledge other sides to the story of groundless student complaints by discussing briefly the behavior of irresponsible instructors and highly responsible students.

Since all the complaints come from my former students, I have tried to establish their complete anonymity. Not only have the students' names been changed in every case, but their gender has been changed in some cases as well. And finally, there is no need to work through the fifteen complaints from beginning to end. The collection may be read in any order the reader wishes.

Gary Colwell
Concordia University College of Alberta
7128 Ada Boulevard
Edmonton, Alberta T5B 4E4

Contents

Acknowledgments

Three of my colleagues at Concordia University College of Alberta deserve special thanks for their contributions to this work. I am very grateful to Timothy McNamara for the conversations we have had together about many of the student complaints discussed in this book. As well, he read the first draft of the manuscript and gave me much encouragement with his written comments. John Woollard also found time in a busy schedule to read and offer critical commentary on the early version. His perspective on the complaints frequently provided a useful contrast to my own. Jonathan Strand was another who was generous with his time as he read parts of the second draft and offered helpful suggestions for its improvement. In addition, I want to thank Sheila Colwell, Bernie Potvin and Zoltan Berkes for kindly reading the second draft and giving me their opinions. To Mary Mahoney-Robson who gave me an important suggestion and to Ted Giles who acted swiftly upon his decision to publish the book I also extend my thanks. However, I do not wish to share any credit for the mistakes that are found in this work. I made them all by myself. At a university college which correctly places a strong emphasis upon teaching it is always a challenge to find time to do research and write. For creating a climate congenial to these multiple pursuits I wish to thank the academic administrators of Concordia, President Richard Kraemer, Vice-President Richard Willie and Dean Catherine Eddy.

1

Complaints About Instructor's Bias

1. "How do I know that you won't indoctrinate us?"

I have discovered in my teaching experience that many students who take university courses have from the outset certain misgivings about their instructors. Their doubts are based upon a preconception which they have formed before ever hearing their instructors lecture. They arrive in class with the belief that instructors have a certain slant on things which students will do well either to avoid, if they do not want their thinking to be warped, or to master, if they wish to earn a good grade. This anxiety about the predominating effects of an instructor's intellectual viewpoint can reveal itself in various ways. One of my clearest examples comes from a student named Jillian who expressed her concerns on the first day of classes in one of my introductory philosophy courses. She wanted to know if I could give her any guarantee that the lectures and arguments that I was going to use in class would be fair and open-minded. For, after all, I had much more knowledge than she, and I could, if I wanted to, use clever but misleading arguments to convince her of things which really she ought not to believe. The influence of my biases could also extend to the grading of student assignments. I might let my point of view blind me to the merits of her work. Her concerns were expressed in the question, "How do I know that you won't indoctrinate us?"

It was clear from the context of our class discussion that she was not attempting to use the word "indoctrinate" in a precise and clear sense. In fact, the vagueness of her use of the word was itself useful, because it incorporated a number of related anxieties which not only she, but other students as well, have about their instructors. Given the context, her question could be interpreted to mean any one or more of the following:

1. perhaps most worrisome of all, because of her instructor's biases, his judgment regarding the merit of her written work might be clouded;

2. because of her instructor's biases and argumentative training, he might take unfair advantage of her in class discussions;

3. because of her instructor's biases, the textual material chosen for the

course might present one-sided views which would not provide her with a balanced education.[1]

The common factor in all the interpretations is the biased nature of the instructor, so I shall try to go to the heart of Jillian's complaint by discussing that first. This will take place in Part A of the analysis which follows. By the end of Part A, interpretation 1 will have been addressed. In Part B I shall address interpretation 2; and in Part C I shall comment briefly on interpretation 3. Before beginning my examination of the biased nature of the instructor, however, I want to say a word about the wider context in which this investigation occurs.

Perceptions of bias which students may have of their instructors are not limited to any particular world view.

Whether a non-religious student encounters a religious instructor or whether a religious student encounters a non-religious instructor, the same kind of worry may emerge: "will the instructor's bias be overbearing so far as my educational development is concerned?"[2] Moreover, the perception that instructors are set in their intellectual ways, to the point of being close-minded and very possibly dangerous, is found not only among students who enroll in what may be called "idea courses," such as philosophy and English, but also among students in the sciences as well. How then should an instructor address such a concern? The issue, like many of those dealt with in this book, is not a simple one; but given its importance, I shall work hard at making the complexity of my answer clear.

Part A: "Biased," "Prejudiced," and "Dogmatic"

Let us begin by drawing a distinction between the meanings of the words *biased*, *prejudiced*, and *dogmatic*.

We cannot appreciate this distinction by adhering strictly to the dictionary definitions of the words. We shall need to sharpen those definitions by making them partly stipulative; that is, by stipulating how the words should be used in order to fully answer Jillian's question.

A bias is a mental tendency or an intellectual slant on a topic. Someone who is *biased* is inclined to think in a certain way about a topic under his consideration. His slanted thinking is the result of his having thought about the topic before, perhaps many times, and forming at least a tentative opinion about it. It is as though by thinking along a certain line, a groove is made in our thought, which is deepened with subsequent thinking. As such, the process of becoming biased with respect to a certain topic cannot be said to be an unusual phenomenon. And because biases are practically unavoidable if we wish to conduct our thinking toward the resolution of a problem, by themselves they can hardly be said to be terrible things.

Take for instance our thinking about the topic of medicare, that is, social insurance for medical care provided by the state. Because of its costliness, some people advocate the complete privatization of medical care. Others, because they believe that certain people of low income would be financially ruined if medical insurance were privatized, object to the proposal. Suppose that you are one who favors maintaining social medical insurance. Likely you have thought about it several times and have an opinion to offer against those who think otherwise. This does not mean that you are unwilling ever to consider arguments which oppose your own; but if you do have a tendency in your thinking about this topic to argue for the maintenance of social medical insurance, you are biased in that direction.

Consider now the instructor who stands before his students ready to give a course of lectures. Such a person today will usually have earned a Ph.D. This means that he or she will have written and defended at least one, and probably two, dissertations. The nature of graduate research is such that people who engage in it adopt positions which they try to defend. It is hard to imagine someone earning a Ph.D. without doing so. The researcher's thinking becomes bent in a certain direction simply in virtue of the nature of the enterprise in which she or he is engaged. Stated briefly, all instructors have developed their biases, and usually quite firm ones at that. And not just about dissertation topics, but also about topics in virtually any area in which they are qualified to teach. Here a note of caution is in order.

If an instructor were to say to me that he or she has no biases or that one of the goals of research and teaching is to clear one's intellectual system of all biases, I would begin to worry. I would worry because the evacuation from one's intellectual system of all tendencies in certain argumentative directions is practically impossible. Furthermore, those who say they have no strong intellectual biases which influence their thinking are usually insensitive to the real undercurrents of their thought, and this insensitivity is the true lurking place of intellectual danger. To use a slightly different metaphor, someone who is aware of his or her biases is less likely to trip over them than someone who is not. This does not imply that an instructor ought always to share his biases with students: indeed, in some cases it is advisable not to do so. Rather, it implies that he should not lecture under the illusion that his thinking is free from biases, nor will he tell his students that he has none. The note of caution to students, then, is this: if your instructor tells you that he has no biases, don't believe him.

I have thought about the influence of biases in college teaching several times before, and have come to the tentative conclusion which I stated in the preceding paragraph. Doesn't this therefore mean that I too am biased, that is, with respect to the topic of bias itself? Yes, I think it does. But the answer to this concern is implied by what I have already said above. However, in the discussion which follows, where I identify the human capacity to achieve critical distance, we shall see more explicitly why this need not always be worrisome.

A *prejudice* is a judgment formed about a topic before an examination of the facts and arguments pertinent to the topic is made.[3] Therefore someone who is *prejudiced* with respect to a particular topic has formed a judgment about that topic before examining the pertinent facts and arguments. Put simply, the prejudiced person *pre-judges* the topic.

According to the dictionary definitions, the person who is *biased* is also said to be *prejudiced*, and vice versa. For purposes of our investigation, however, I would prefer not to say that they are strictly synonymous. This is because I would like us to think of the *prejudiced* person as holding a view on a topic more firmly that the person who is *biased*. This greater firmness of belief may result from overconfidence with respect to a topic, due to the fact that the overconfident person has examined the topic many times before from many different angles and has come to a solid opinion about it; or, it may derive from an emotional association which has been set up between the person's (prejudiced) thinking and the topic; or, perhaps a mixture of both. According to this stipulative definition, all prejudiced people are biased, but not all biased people are prejudiced.

Consider again the topic of medicare. According to my stipulative definition, the biased supporter of social medical insurance is inclined to think along certain lines and to proffer certain arguments on behalf of retaining it. But being inclined in a certain direction does not mean that he will prejudge the arguments of his opponents before hearing them. The biased supporter may say something like, "I'm in favor of retaining medicare, for the following reasons, A, B, and C; but the speaker might have a persuasive argument which I haven't yet considered; I'm willing to listen to her and consider it." By contrast, the prejudiced supporter may say something like, "I've thought it through carefully and I'm in favor of retaining medicare; I'll listen to her speech, but there really isn't much point; it will be the same old conservative views I've heard before."

If, however, the supporter of medicare is *dogmatic*, he will hold his view with a firmness that exceeds even that of the *prejudiced* supporter. His certainty about the rightness of his opinion will be marked by an authoritative pronouncement. It may go something like this: "I know that

I'm right because it is the only sensible position; you asked me to listen to her speech and I did, reluctantly; and even though I cannot refute some of her main arguments now, in time I will be able to do so; I know that they must be wrong because retaining medicare is the only sensible position." One of the dangers that a person faces in adopting a dogmatic stance with respect to a topic is that he is liable to fall into fallacious circular reasoning when defending his view of the topic.[4]

Before we can directly address Jillian's concern about the predominating influence of her instructor's ideas, we must push our investigation a little further. For it is not sufficient to observe that we can hold a view on a topic with varying degrees of firmness. We need also to recognize that we can mentally distance ourselves from our own view, however firmly we hold it. We can stand back from it, so to speak, and take a look at it. From there we can choose to let our view, however firmly held, close our minds to the merits of an opposing view, or we can choose to open our minds to the possible merits of an opposing view. Adopting the second choice is like holding our own view at arm's length with our left hand, while inspecting the opposing view with our right hand. It would seem perfectly coherent to me if the supporter of medicare were to say, "I realize that I am biased in favor of retaining medicare, but I will not let my slant on the topic spoil my judgment of the speaker's argument for abolishing it."

The essential point is this: the firmness with which a view is held is one matter; an unwillingness to detach oneself from the firmly held view, in order to evaluate an opposing view, is another matter; and the two ought not to be confused. Unfortunately, confusion does exist, and its existence can be found embedded in the dictionary definitions of those words which relate directly to our subject.

In speaking about the human capacity to stand back from our slanted views, and not be absorbed by them, we are speaking about our ability to be *objective* or *dispassionate*. However, if we look up the word *objective* in the dictionary we shall find that one of its meanings is *unbiased*. And if we look up the word *dispassionate* we shall find the same result, because one of its meanings is also *free from bias*.

Because the words *objective*, *dispassionate* and *unbiased* are defined as synonyms, and hence, because the words *dispassionate* and *biased* are seen as antonyms, according to the dictionary one cannot be both biased and dispassionate (or objective). But this just seems to be untrue. The definitions do not capture the important difference which does in fact exist between the capacity to hold a view with a certain degree of firmness or confidence, on the one hand, and the ability to detach oneself from that view in order to assess an opposing view, on the other hand. Dictionaries do a good job at making rough and ready definitions, and often their definitions are suitably precise, but sometimes what the definitions imply is plainly false. That, I believe, is the case with the definitions of *objective* and *bias*.

A lack of appreciation for the human capacity for intellectual self-detachment may account for a number of questions and comments which an instructor hears from students every year in nearly every course. A common question is, "What do you want on this essay?" Such a question can be a sincere desire to understand better the instructions on the essay assignment sheet; but more often than not it is about what the student perceives to be the secret slant on the essay topic which only the instructor has. If the student can gently pry it out of him with a question then he can begin his work with a measure of confidence. No matter how clear or detailed the instructions are, some student will feel that unless he uncovers the bias of his instructor he will run a grave risk in writing the essay using only his research material and best judgment.

Other comments by students also reveal the preconception about biases which we have been at pains to analyse. Students will often say of their instructors, "he didn't like my essay" or "he didn't care for my ideas." In such cases the student does not say, "he criticized my essay for being off the topic, ungrammatical, disorganized or incoherent." Rather, they say "he didn't like my essay." It seems that some students believe that, when it comes to student essays, their instructors have likes and dislikes which may be compared to tastes, with the taste buds for essays being the instructor's biases. The preconception is strong and pervasive that his biases really are at the root of all his criticisms.[5]

This claim about intellectual self-detachment may sound convincing if applied to a biased view; but can it hold for a dogmatic view as well? Can a person be both dogmatic with respect to his own view and open to the possible merits of someone else's opposing view? Our intellectual reflexes react against such a possibility. But notice why. Largely it is because we have imbibed a definition of *dogmatism* which precludes such a possibility. In our thinking we have grown used to equating firmness (or confidence) of belief with the inability to detach ourselves from that belief. I am arguing, however, that such an equation cannot truly be made.

There may, however, be a case to be made for the claim that it becomes more difficult to detach oneself from one's own view, in order to assess fairly an opposing view, as one's own view becomes increasingly more firmly held. Presumably, as one moves from being *biased* to being *prejudiced* to being *dogmatic* about one's own view, as well as an opposing view, one finds it increasingly difficult to be objective about the opposing view. However, I am not even sure that this is true. But let us make the assumption for the sake of argument, namely, that in all cases it happens to be true. It still would not follow that it *has* to be true. It may have been the case that the dogmatists have simply not developed their capacity for critical self-detachment. They can easily enough open their minds to opposing views while very firmly holding onto their own, but they choose not to do so. Perhaps one reason for not doing so is intellectual laziness. It is just more comfortable not to have to be bothered with assessing opposing views. Perhaps another reason is fear. It could turn out that the opposing view is better than one's own; that, of course, would bring another kind of uneasiness which the unobjective dogmatist may want to avoid.

But notice that laziness and fear are different from the supposed lack of intellectual capacity to distance oneself from one's own view. There is nothing intrinsic to the firmness of a belief which makes objectivity about opposing beliefs impossible. The close-mindedness which almost always is associated with bias, prejudice and dogmatism is produced, not by increasing the firmness of one's grip on the view being held, but, rather, from an unwillingness to hold the firmly gripped view at arm's length long enough to evaluate an opposing view in the other hand. The motives for this close-mindedness are no doubt several in number, two of which have been identified above. Whatever specifically they are, generally speaking they may be said to produce a meanness of spirit or attitude, a lack of generosity in outlook. What a student like Jillian needs to worry about, therefore, is not so much the firmness with which an instructor holds a view, but, instead, the lack of generosity of spirit which prevents him from seeing the merit of an opposing view.

One of the ways in which an instructor can allay the fears of students who worry about not getting a fair hearing is to demonstrate, with examples, what I have just been arguing. In my experience, social ethics courses produce some of the most heated discussions of any philosophy course in the curriculum. This is because the philosophical problems which are discussed in such courses are live ones for most of the students. How could they not be when the media are all ablaze with discussions of reproductive technology, euthanasia, abortion, capital punishment (among others). But as well, many students have enrolled in such courses to find answers to these pressing problems, or at least to find intellectual support for their adopted answers. Indeed in class discussions I find that students will share personal accounts from their own experiences which bear directly on the ethical issue under discussion. Given their emotional attachment to certain answers which they have adopted as a result of dealing with these ethical problems at home or at work or with a friend in difficulty, their concern with the instructor's slant on issues is magnified. What I like to do therefore is give them some encouraging statistics about past student performance and refer them to papers on reserve in the library.

Last semester, for example, in my social ethics course I had four excellent students who earned a final grade of 9, the highest score possible on the stanine system used by my university college. At the beginning of this semester's lectures in the same course I informed the new class that three of the four students last semester consistently disagreed with my views on the topics under discussion. So, although one student shared my biases, the remaining three did not, and in fact frequently opposed them; yet all four students got top marks. Critical questions might be raised at this point by someone who is cynical about the value of such an exercise, but at least this much can be established: a student does not have to agree with the instructor to get an outstanding grade. I do the same with essays throughout the term. I place on reserve in the library three or four excellent ones which display a range of different viewpoints with respect to the same class assignment.

We can now directly address Jillian's concern about prejudicial blindness by summarizing our conclusions. Just because an instructor is biased with respect to a particular topic, it does not mean that he is prejudiced about it. And if he is prejudiced, it does not follow that he is dogmatic. But even if he were prejudiced or dogmatic that would still not mean that he could not be objective. A student like Jillian may take some encouragement from the fact that her instructor's training in philosophy (or other discipline) will usually have required him to explore the alternative points of view with respect to nearly every topic which he has seriously examined. That training helps to foster the habit of adopting a critical detachment with respect to his students' work.

It would be irresponsibly naive to paint a picture of university and college teaching in which *every* instructor, with spontaneous generosity, looks for the merit of his students' arguments, irrespective of the firmness of his own opinions on the topic under discussion. I personally have not encountered such universal magnanimity, either in my own graduate training, or in the reports from former students who have pursued graduate work. Earning a Ph.D. does not automatically transform a graduate student into a generous and open-minded instructor with respect to arguments opposing his own. Such generosity cannot simply be pre-programmed, no matter how good the graduate training is. If an instructor does not already possess a generous disposition, but wants to become generous in his dealings with students, he will have to decide deliberately to become generous; and this implies a fair amount of self-vigilance and hard work. However, what I think I can say with confidence is that any graduate training which consistently encourages the examination of alternative sides of an issue helps to promote a spirit of openness.[6]

It is evident, therefore, that we cannot answer Jillian's question in such a way that she may have complete trust in her instructor *before* she actually takes the course. With respect to guaranteeing her the objectivity which she is so anxious to know exists in the mind of her instructor, a less than completely satisfying answer must be given. She will simply have to wait and see. But now at least she has some good reasons for giving him the benefit of the doubt, initially. She knows that her instructor's greater knowledge and experience, as well as his slant on the topics on which he lectures, do not *by themselves* mean that he cannot be open-minded about the merit of her performance in the course. And this will be the case even when she disagrees with her instructor.

There is another side to this question of bias, prejudice and dogmatism which, in a perverse way, may give a student like Jillian added comfort. Not only are instructors biased, but so also are their students. If students find the rigidity of their instructors' views worrisome, their instructors are no less troubled by the incorrigibility of their students. It is not uncommon for an instructor to read examination answers which are totally oblivious to those extended discussions in class which exposed the weakness of such answers. And here I am not talking about students who were absent from class when the discussions took place or were daydreaming in class. These are students who heard and understood the discussions but chose to hold onto their answers anyway. Even as an instructor may remain committed to his views throughout the course, so, a student may do likewise. Of course the reasons, or lack thereof, for the unshaken commitments may vary from instructor to student.

However, just as it is possible for an instructor to remain open to the merits of a student's idea which is inferior to his own, so it is possible for a student to remain closed to the merits of an instructor's idea which is superior to his own. And this is because the same non-rational factors are at work in both cases, ones which bear upon the mechanism of self-detatchment. It may be activated by us at will, provided we are also willing to engage in self-denial. Students like Jillian can observe this by using empathy and introspection. And in making their observations they can see that the instructor's greater knowledge, wider experience and established biases, by themselves, should not be a cause for worry; they will not blind him to the merits of a student's work.

Part B: Playing the Devil's Advocate

With the foundation of our discussion of biases in place, we can deal with interpretations 2 and 3 more quickly. Regarding Jillian's concern (2), that her instructor might take unfair advantage of her lack of philosophical training during class discussions, we can repeat the observation we made in Part A. Just because an instructor has a more mature view on a topic than the one which the student expresses in class, that does not mean that the instructor cannot see the merit of the student's viewpoint. For even if he disagrees with his student and offers a criticism of her position, he can still recognize, for example, that for a first-year student she has advanced an insightful and thought-provoking argument. And if he is a good teacher he will tell her so. There is no necessary incompatibility, therefore, between an instructor "winning" an argument with a student during class discussions and, at the same time, recognizing the real merit of the student's ideas. His biases need not get in the way of his objective evaluations.

A tried and tested method which instructors use to train their students in argumentation is called "playing the devil's advocate." The historical origin of the phrase is interesting and instructive in this context. We must go back to the fifteenth and sixteenth centuries, to the reigns of pope Leo X and pope Sixtus V. In the Roman Catholic Church a deceased person may be proposed as a candidate for beatification or canonization. His or her name may be put forward to the pope to be declared blessed or to be counted among the company of the New Testament saints. In 1587 Sixtus V formally established an office to examine the qualifications of such candidates. The person holding the office was responsible for critically examining the life and miracles attributed to the nominated candidates. The presentation of his findings included everything unfavorable to the candidate. This critical examiner was known as the *advocatus diaboli* (devil's advocate) because, presumably, the Church wanted to be assured that the candidate's record could stand the scrutiny of even the most hostile adversary, one sent by the devil himself. The "devil's advocate" was also known as "the promoter of the faith," again presumably because his critical scrutiny saved the Church from making a sham of the faith, that is, from making claims of worthiness about a candidate who was actually unworthy.[7]

In a similar way, an instructor may critically examine a student's argument, not necessarily because he doesn't think that the argument is a worthy one, but because he wants to see if the student can show that it is. Can it withstand close scrutiny? Having an instructor play the devil's advocate by presenting objections to even those views which he believes to be true is important to a student's intellectual growth. Indeed, this process of sifting arguments for elements of lasting value is important to everyone's intellectual growth.

The qualification about not being naive, which was made in our discussion of interpretation 1, applies here equally well. In the classroom, as well as in the instructor's study, it is possible for intellectual insecurity and mean-spiritedness to predominate. But the proper response to this possibility is also the same as the one above. I know of no way that a student can be completely certain that a instructor will not take unfair argumentative advantage of her before she actually enrolls in the course. Of course a student can always ask around, as many of them do. Just as students have a grapevine for discovering bargains on good used books, so they have a grapevine for passing along their informal ratings of instructors. There are a couple of difficulties with this approach, however. An instructor's classroom behavior can't be inspected before the student actually enrolls in his course. And equally confounding is the fact that what seem like intimidating or otherwise off putting characteristics to one student will not seem so to another student. Student responses to an instructor's style of teaching and personality can vary widely, as termly evaluations repeatedly show.

If this account sounds unduly pessimistic and unpromising to the student reader, or to any reader, for that matter, it shouldn't. I am trying to present a realistic picture of the instructor which makes him appear not better and not worse than people in other professions or occupations. For example, the automotive mechanic who works on your car can "snow" you with technical terms and a bleak scenario about what your car needs to keep its wheels from falling off. He *can* use his superior knowledge and biases about what constitutes a well-running car to take unfair advantage of you. But he need not do so, and we trust that most mechanics do not. But *if* he does, it will not be his expertise which is the cause of the unfair advantage taking; it will be something more fundamental and pervasive about his character. The same may be said about your member of parliament, your minister or priest, and yes, even your best friend. All of these people can deliberately use their expertise to convince you of things which they know they have no warrant to say, in order to get you to believe or do what they want you to do. But again, they need not do so. And whether or not they do, has little, if anything, to do with their expertise. Charitability and a generosity of spirit will not be hampered by superior knowledge and argumentative skills.

To summarize interpretation 2, then, an instructor's criticism of his student's argument does not necessarily mean that he thinks little of the argument or that his low opinion of the argument, if he holds such an opinion, is due to his personal biases. It may well mean that he is engaged in his proper business of challenging the student to think harder about what she has said. A student should therefore expect to receive critical questions and objections from her instructor and not assume at the outset that they proceed from dubious motives. Nor is there reason to think that because an instructor has expertise which his student does not have, he will take unfair advantage of the student; or at least as little reason for thinking this as one would have for thinking it about any other class of professional people.[8]

Part C: On Choosing a Text

We are left with interpretation 3, the concern that an instructor's bias may lead him to choose textual material which is one-sided. I have already argued that instructors, to some extent, are products of their training. But I have also observed above that, although an instructor's previous academic influences could turn out to be cause for worry, they need not be so. Much depends upon the intellectual generosity, or lack thereof, of the instructor. The same observations apply to the concern at hand.

There is little that is random about an instructor's choice of texts. More often than not he will have found one or more texts which, as far as the material, the approach, and the arguments are concerned, agree with his biases about how such a course should be conducted. But to say that the material agrees with his biases about how the course should conducted is different from saying that all the textual material he chooses agrees with his formed opinions about the subject matter he wants his students to investigate.

Rather, the instructor will probably choose a text which contains much material which disagrees with his own opinions. How this can happen has already been discussed. Of course he can take refuge in "safe" material, and I suppose that this is sometimes done; but once again he is not forced to do so because of his biases. By themselves they will not blind him to the intellectual merit of opinions contrary to his own.

One very important factor should not be lost sight of in all our talk of biases: some of the material which an instructor must cover in the humanities is standard. One simply cannot offer a course in the major dialogues of Plato without placing the *Republic* on the reading list. Nor can one study modern empiricism in any depth without studying the work of David Hume. To take a different discipline, one cannot offer a course in the major plays of Shakespeare without having students read *Hamlet* or *King Lear*. And while it is true there are different translations of the *Republic* and different editorial introductions to different editions of Shakespeare's work, the degree to which these factors alone will prejudice a student's education is not likely to be significant.

There is yet another dimension to our discussion of the alleged biases of an instructor which we must not overlook. An instructor ought to be able to assume that he has in his classes, not just passive sponges, but rather, active minds. Without this assumption colleges and universities may as well close their doors. Some effort will have to be made, and should be expected to be made, by the students themselves to evaluate the material they receive, even if their ability to evaluate it is, understandably, still immature.

Here again it would be naive to expect that most beginning students can maturely assess their instructors' biases and separate the intellectual wheat from the chaff. Still, it is not clear that they need to be able to do this at the beginning of their university program in order to receive a good education. Moreover, they can take some comfort in the fact that further training received in subsequent courses will increase their ability to evaluate the arguments they hear. Of course instructors have an important part to play in this training process. One of our major tasks, especially if we are philosophy instructors, is to help students develop their thinking skills so they can accurately detect their instructors' biases and critically evaluate their views.

Just as we grow up and modify some of the things we were taught in our youth, so, as we move through the university system, we can modify or even abandon some of the ideas we heard earlier, if, under analysis, they no longer seem right. Just as Rome was not built in a day, a university education will not be completed by taking one course.[9]

2

Excuses and Complaints About Essays

2. "Why my essay is late."

"You won't believe this, but..."

The most inventive excuse I have ever heard for not getting an essay in on time comes from a young man who took a course from me in 1988. The course was called Introduction to Western Philosophy which involved a discussion of some of the classic texts of ancient, modern and contemporary philosophers. Michael approached me after class on Monday, the day on which the essay was due, and said: "You won't believe this, but, I left my essay in my typewriter, and my typewriter was in the trunk of my car, which was in the garage over the weekend being fixed. Therefore, I couldn't complete my essay, and that's why I can't pass it in today." My first and lasting response was, "you're right I don't believe it." Michael no doubt detected a tinge of incredulity in my response, so he proceeded to explain his way into this odd situation. He said that he had first intended to get his typewriter fixed, put it into his trunk, drove around for awhile, but then experienced serious car trouble and had to take it to a garage. Apparently this was late on Friday. During the course of depositing his car with the garage mechanic he forgot about his typewriter. And since it was Friday and his essay wasn't due until Monday he wasn't especially concerned with completing his essay in a hurry, so he also forgot about its being in his typewriter. Only after he left the garage did he remember the typewriter and the essay, at which time it was too late to retrieve them.

Michael's knitted brow and general seriousness while he recounted this unlikely episode made me, as they say, "half-believe" him. I started to think that this is just the sort of story which could be true. No one could make this up, I thought. Stereotypical thinking started to possess me and I began to say to myself, "fact is stranger than fiction." But then this thinking was met with scepticism as I remembered the reports I had heard about the psychologically gripping power of what World War II historians have called "The Big Lie."

I think that what ultimately pulled me out of my quandary was my inability to make the pieces of Michael's story fit a coherent pattern. And his responses to my puzzlement exacerbated the problem instead of alleviating it. For example, I never did get from him a satisfactory reason for his essay being in his typewriter. Why would anyone have several pages in a typewriter at once; and why would he leave them there when he was taking the typewriter in for repairs? And if there was only one page in the typewriter, how could he legitimately say that he left his essay there? And if he was so near the beginning of his essay why did he not start again, write it out in long-hand and then show me that at least he had completed it? (The reader can see that being an instructor these days is not easy business.) As interesting as these questions may be to ponder, we must turn our attention to the central question of how best to deal with student excuses for turning in essays late.

Here is the context within which the excuses for late submissions must be entertained. The essay assignment sheet has been distributed to the students, well in advance of the due date for the essay; in my classes this means at least a month and often two months before the essay is due. The students are required to produce a typescript and have been encouraged to get to work on their assignment right away. The penalty for late essays has been clearly stated and a rider has been attached to the statement. It reads like this: "only in circumstances considered by your instructor to be exceptional will this penalty be waived, and then only with his prior approval." Which circumstances should I consider to be exceptional and what criteria shall I use to decide? If there is anything that I have discovered about setting forth clear conditions for submitting essays, it is this: no matter how specific one tries to be, it is highly unlikely that all contingencies will or can be covered. Occasionally a student will arrive at my office door with an account of an unheard-of circumstance which at first glance seems to provide her with a warrant for not meeting the deadline for essay submissions. In short, there is ultimately no substitute for making informed judgments, even if sometimes they are ad hoc judgments. The excuse which I have just related is one of the easier ones with which I have had to deal. The next three are not so easy, and their resolutions seem to me to be of progressively increasing difficulty.

"My typewriter ribbon broke."

Betty and her classmates had been instructed to bring their essays to class on the due date. On that day she came to my office slightly agitated just before the class began. She informed me that, because her typewriter ribbon had broken the night before, she could not pass in her essay on time; and she asked me if I would give her an extension until the following morning. (There was no evidence in her account to lead me to believe that she did anything to remove the impediment. She did not, for instance, scout around for a new ribbon or typewriter.) Betty's late-essay excuse is typical and occurs fairly frequently. It belongs to a larger class of excuses which we could call "excuses based upon material or mechanical failure." Variations run like this: "my printer gave out just last night," "my car broke down on my way to class," "there was a fire in my cell block and my essay got burned up," and so on.

One of the positive things that we can say about Betty's excuse is that it is easier to digest than Michael's. The breaking of a typewriter ribbon is a relatively common occurrence. Though one does wonder about the rate at which certain coincidences connected with such breaks occur: why do so many breaks occur on just the night before an essay is due? (Appealing to Murphy's Law will not, unfortunately, help us here; because it isn't a law and it doesn't explain anything.) In all events, Betty's excuse seems at first glance to be a plausible one and to warrant the granting of an extension. But we need to take a second look at this because first glances can be misleading.

Two themes will be dominant in our consideration of student excuses, and these will apply to Betty's excuse as well:
1. fairness to other members of the class, and
2. time management skills.

Regarding the first theme, we need to ask whether it is fair to other members of the class to allow Betty to have an extension when the others managed to work successfully under the same time constraints. We might well reason that probably at least one other person encountered a malfunction in some piece of equipment or a depletion of some material which was necessary to her completing the assignment. And yet she may have overcome the obstacle at great personal cost and energy. For instance, if her printer quit working, she may have prevailed upon a service technician to give her printer priority, which in turn may well have meant that she had to make several phone calls and drive long distances. If it was too late to have the machine serviced, she may have prevailed upon one of her friends to loan her a printer or even to do the typing for her. Along the same line, perhaps she paid someone whose name had been on one of the campus bulletin boards to do a rush job for a heavy price. And other possibilities can easily and realistically be imagined.

It may well be a fact that one or more members of the class sacrificed a significant amount of time or money or energy, or all three, to meet the essay deadline. And should we not at least ask the other members of the class what their stories are before we make a judgment on Betty's case. We see here again, as we shall see in the section on the appeal to authority, how certain actions, which seem so reasonable when considered in isolation from their realistic contexts, are completely impractical when placed within their appropriate life-situations. Just imagine the time that would be consumed on the day when each assignment was to be passed in – and quite possibly the following "who-knows-how-many?" days.

But perhaps the actual fact of the others' self-sacrifice in meeting the deadline is not the most basic point to be considered in this discussion. Whether anyone actually did have to give a great deal more of herself than normally would be required, were everything working smoothly, should not be the decisive factor. The point is that the instructor has a right to expect that she will make such a sacrifice if something like a malfunctioning printer requires her to do so.

"Even an unreasonable sacrifice?" someone may be inclined to ask. And the natural follow-up question is: how does one determine what a reasonable sacrifice is? I do not know what the necessary and sufficient conditions are which will enable us to distinguish a reasonable sacrifice from an unreasonable one. But perhaps we do not need to know that much in order to make a sensible judgment. Likely something less will suffice than having to produce the universally applicable criteria for isolating cases of rational self-sacrifice under conditions of impending assignment due dates. G.E. Moore has taught us that we do not need to be able to define exhaustively a chair in order to be able to recognize one when we see it. Similarly, we do not need to be able to state with precision what all the conditions are for distinguishing a reasonable self-sacrifice from an unreasonable one when contemplating the meaning of a broken type-writer ribbon on the night before our essay is due. Given our knowledge of human capabilities and of available resources in a fairly large city, we have enough models of behavior upon which to draw in order to make our assessment. Certainly the examples which we have given are not excessive in their expectations, that is, not unreasonable. And surely Betty could have been expected to try a bit harder to overcome her obstacle to success. That is, it is not unreasonable of us to expect her to have tried to do so. If, however, the local fire chief had phoned me on the day before the essay was due and informed me that on that day Betty's house and all its contents had been destroyed by fire, including Betty's typewriter and essay, then that failure of materials would be a somewhat stronger reason to grant her an extension.

But what if Betty's ribbon breaks at 2:30 a.m. on the morning that the essay is due, just as she is beginning to type page number five of a seven-page essay? Is she supposed to phone around town at that hour of the morning? As a preliminary answer to this question, let me surmise that many, if not most instructors upon seeing Betty's four typed pages together with her completed hand-written draft would grant her a day's extension. The answer that goes to the heart of the question, however, pertains to the priority of expectations which an instructor may reasonably be said to have of his or her students, including Betty. If a student is in a position of needing to make an unreasonable self-sacrifice in order to get her assignment in on time, and this is due to her poor planning, is not this unhappy situation her responsibility? Has she not created the need to make such unreasonable self-demands in order to meet the deadline. We may state a general rule on the question of the reasonableness and priority of an instructor's expectation: expectations of planning supersede expectations of self-sacrifice. Put sharply, was it not possible for Betty to plan to finish her essay a day or two before the due date, with just this idea in mind, that if something were to go wrong in the final stages of producing her essay, she would have ample time to correct it and meet the deadline? In fact, here again, may we not assume that at least some of her classmates did use this very approach in producing their essays? And if so, would it not be unfair to give Betty an extension when by forethought and industry her classmates showed that none was needed?

"I got the flu."

This is a more convincing excuse than "my typewriter broke." First, because illness is more serious than mechanical or material failure, and it touches each of us personally. We do not need to have overly vivid imaginations to remember how *we* felt when we were dragging our bones around and trying to accomplish mundane tasks, let alone special tasks like writing a creative term paper.

Moreover, it seems to be a more believable excuse because it occurs more frequently. If there is anything that an instructor can count on it is that sickness will increase and attendance will decrease as the academic year wears on. What is an instructor to do, then, when a student phones in sick or appears at his office door red-eyed and wanting an extension on her essay?

Here is where three pertinent factors come into play at once: fairness, planning, and the need for good judgment. It seems to me that one cannot make a decision on this matter without asking a few questions. If today is the due date for the essay, did she contract the flu yesterday? And if she had it all week, has she been able to do any intellectual work at all? And if so, for what period of time? In other words, is this a mild case of the flu or a serious case; has it occurred recently or has it been protracted? I do not think that most instructors enjoy playing physician-detective; but without a willingness to play that role to a minor extent, a more rough and ready approach will have to be used. It will have to be either something like, "Oh sure, no problem, how much time do you need?" or like, "That's tough, but you have had over a month to research and write a seven-page paper." While I have more sympathies for the second approach than the first, I am not sure that it is a fair one. What makes it especially difficult to live with is the appearance of a student at the office door with a note from a physician saying that Cynthia has been confined to bed for the past week. And while an instructor is not being unreasonable to be firm in assessing reported cases of flu which pop up on the day before the essay is due, he is probably being unreasonable to expect the flu victim to have been so well-organized that she completed her essay one week in advance of the due date. But what if the student says that she contracted the flu only three days ago? I repeat, judgment is required; and here there are likely to be differences of opinion. To avoid an unwelcome encounter with a seemingly unsympathetic instructor, a student who catches the flu, and has early warning signals that it is likely to be a prolonged illness, is advised to notify him immediately. Then, when she stands before him three days later, red-eyed and dizzy, asking for an extension, the request will be much more convincing. Before concluding, a couple of qualifications are in order.

Some students choose to work on assignments or to write final exams under conditions of quite serious physical illness. I know of one student who chose to write three of his mid-term exams while suffering from a severe case of the flu. His reluctance to ask for a postponement was based upon the thinking that, although he would not have to write his exams under the adverse influence of the flu, he would have to write make-up exams a week or two later under circumstances which on balance might not be any better, and could conceivably be worse. He reasoned that, in two weeks' time he would have to work extra hard to get his knowledge up to the level where it was when he caught the flu; besides which, other assignments demanding his attention would have piled up during the interim and placed him under added stress.

At some large universities and colleges the niceties of argumentation about individual flu cases which we have been entertaining here may be quite foreign to the policy of an instructor or teaching assistant. So, once again, it is advised that the student learn the rules, or lack thereof, of her institution early in her academic career.

In the final analysis, a student may be expected to plan his research and writing schedule in such a way as to be able to contend with mild cases of illness should they occur "at the last minute." In many cases of severe illness a student naturally will not be able to complete his assignment on time. But even if the illness is protracted, say for a week or more, time management and academic planning will make these adverse circumstances much easier to recover from than otherwise would be the case. Concerning those cases of illness which fall between the extremes of being mild and being severe, so far as I can see, unless an instructor is going to adopt either an approach which says "accept every excuse" or "reject every excuse" he will have to make a judgment based upon answers to some basic questions about the illness itself.

"My grandmother died."

Whereas reported mechanical failures are likely to elicit little support for a request to have a due date extended, and flu cases are more likely to gain the sympathy of an instructor, a reported death in the family will probably make the strongest impression of all. This is especially so if a close relative such as a parent or a sibling has died. There is little question when such an unfortunate event occurs that it will have a profound and adverse effect upon almost any student. An excellent student of mine reported to me that her brother had committed suicide; then she took a week off from classes to recuperate from the shock. Sadly, she never did recover the academic ground she had gained before the tragedy, and her grades plummeted sharply. Acknowledging that such an event can make a dramatic difference in a student's performance, including the ability to get assignments in on time, is there really any need to discuss further the reported deaths of family members?

Like a number of other excuses that students offer for not getting assignments in on time, a reported death in the family is not always a clear-cut issue either. An important factor to be considered is the closeness of the relationship which the student has had with the deceased. We have already suggested that in the case of a reported death of a parent or sibling there is nothing to discuss as far as granting an extension is concerned. But what about the death of a cousin? Or, as is more common, what about the death of a grandmother?

My colleagues at Concordia have recently reported an increase in the number of dead-grandmother excuses being used for a variety of requested extensions. Perhaps nearly all the excuses are legitimate. However, an instructor will tend to become sceptical after learning through the faculty grapevine that the same student has suffered the loss of three grandmothers in one semester.

The question remains, though, is there anything an instructor can do, or ought to do, when he hears from a student that his grandmother has died and he receives a request for an extension on his essay — other that simply granting the extension? Frankly, I don't think so.

An informed judgment in this case could best be made if the instructor could get some basic answers to some basic questions about how close the student was to her grandmother. For it would make a difference in his judgment to know whether, for example, her grandmother had raised her and had been a part of her immediate family, or whether, by contrast, her grandmother had lived in Europe all her life and was hardly known to her. However, the main problem with trying to make such an informed judgment in this case concerns the matter of propriety. An instructor would seem to be callous and mildly disrespectful if he were to query a student about her relationship to her grandmother. And for this reason he would not usually tread upon that ground. Unfortunately, the respectful attitude which an instructor may properly be expected to adopt can be made to work against his purposes. An insincere student, if there were such, who had had a very distant relationship with her grandmother, might conceivably use the situation of her grandmother's death to gain more time to do her essay, when in truth none was needed. Even to suggest such a thing, I know, borders on the irreverent; but occasionally one may find a student whose motive for requesting an extension on the basis of a relative's death isn't entirely pure.

Perhaps the best that can be done in this situation is to offer the student condolences and encourage her not to put off completing the essay too long. Having her set the new due date, within a reasonable time, would also be an appropriate response.

3. "I spent 20 hours on this essay."

This complaint came from Thomas who was unhappy and genuinely puzzled about the grade he received on his essay. Contributing to his puzzlement was the fact that his friend William, who spent about four hours on his essay, and wrote it the night before it was due, got a higher mark than he did. Thomas seemed to think that because he had worked very hard on his essay he was deserving of a much better grade; that one's grade should increase in proportion to the time one spends, no matter who the student may be. The fallacy in his thinking is this: *effort alone is enough to get a student a good grade.*

This is a misconception about the relationship between work, talent and grades which will be dealt with in detail in Chapter 3, and particularly in my discussion of complaints 5, 6, and 8. But a few general comments here will give the reader an idea of what is to come.

It ought to be clearly evident to all students, but unfortunately isn't for some, that not just the quantity of work which one does is significant in the business of getting good grades, but also the quality of work as well. Perhaps we can frame a principle which will provide a general answer to the puzzlement found in this complaint above: *hard work is a necessary but not a sufficient condition for getting good grades.* The ability to handle the ideas and concepts which characterize a discipline must also be given the weight it deserves. In the discussions found in Chapter 3, I shall make some observations about the importance of possessing at least some talent for a subject if one expects to earn a good grade in it. And, of course, ability alone is not enough either. The absence of a full realization of this fact may be largely responsible for several of the complaints that follow.

4. "My mother is an English teacher – she liked my essay."

It is common for students to complain about the marks they get on their essays. One type of complaint which an instructor hears at least once or twice in an academic year can be classified as *an appeal to an inappropriate authority.* An example which I heard from a student named Waldo goes like this: "my mother is an English teacher; she read my essay and thought that it was very good; she said that I certainly didn't deserve the low grade I got."

Here temptations abound. One would like to say to Waldo, "sometimes joy can be found in reading sub-standard work," or alternatively, "you should take your mother's course; it will be an easier three credits." Although these responses may have merit, I am inclined to think that "fighting fire with fire" in this case is not going to be in the best interests of the student. The best approach, if the student will permit the instructor to use it, is just to ignore the appeal, go directly to the essay and explain specifically what its shortcomings are. I have found that students are usually satisfied with this approach. But what if Waldo had not been not satisfied with this approach and persisted in dragging in his mother's expertise to justify his unhappiness and give warrant to his claim that he should receive a higher mark? This I surmise would be a rare occurrence, for it has not happened in my experience or in the reported experiences of my close associates, though I have heard of it occurring in the experiences of other colleagues.

My closest encounter with this type of reaction came when a student named Sharon brought me a letter from her father in which he complained about the mark which my grading assistant had put on his daughter's essay. The letter began: "I am astonished at the failure mark awarded Sharon. . . ." I was immediately alerted to the possibility that Sharon's father might not be an English teacher. The body of the letter ended with the observation that my grading assistant had ignored the viewpoint which the instructions on my essay assignment sheet had clearly stated. "I believe that viewpoint has been ignored by an existentialist bias and that elementary semantic truths were disallowed." Then it also occurred to me that Sharon's father may not have been burdened with the study of large amounts of philosophy during his formal academic training.

For the record, only a few times in my experience have I used a grading assistant. And my grading assistant on this occasion was Janet who had nearly finished her Ph.D. in philosophy and was being sponsored in her effort by a government research grant, a highly competitive award which was very difficult to secure. Although I did not respond to Sharon's father's letter, I did re-mark her essay, and my judgment was even less generous than Janet's. As enlightening as the remaining details of that story might be, we must return to the question facing us. Whether or not the student permits his instructor to ignore his appeal to an external authority, what rationale does the instructor have for doing so? What *should* one say about Waldo's "my-mother-is-an-English-teacher" argument?

Let us be positive in our approach. This is a much better argument than, say, "my mother is a fighter pilot who has studied aeronautical engineering and flown many missions, and she says that I've written a good essay." On the face of it, the English-teacher argument is more relevant to the matter of assessing the grade on a philosophy essay than is the fighter-pilot argument. But is it relevant enough to warrant a change in the instructor's judgment regarding the grade he has given a student's essay? And more importantly, is the question of the relevance of the outside authority's expertise itself even relevant? In other words, should the relevance which the outside authority's expertise has to the instructor's assessment even be taken as significant when considering what to do with a student's appeal to such an authority? Let us take the questions one at a time.

Arguments from authority are sometimes fallacious, and when they are, they fall within the general class of fallacies called *fallacies of irrelevance.* When an appeal is made to an authority whose expertise is not in the subject on behalf of which the appeal is made, then the appeal is irrelevant, and consequently the argument which uses the appeal is fallacious. Of course advertisers, as well as students, use such arguments, the former more deliberately than the latter, we hope. And while it is not logically convincing that Shutterblast cameras are dependable just because some famous hockey player endorses them on television, advertisers know that setting up an association in the minds of viewers, between the famous hockey player and Shutterblast cameras, will sell the cameras far more effectively than evidence and logic will. Similarly, Waldo seemed to think that his appeal to his mother's expertise in teaching English would create a positive association in my mind between his mother's authority and the quality of his essay. "But perhaps Waldo was justified in making such an appeal," it might be asked.

One of the factors which makes the question of an appeal to authority complicated is the matter of the degree to which the authority is relevant. Quite a few times in my career I have listened to students appeal to their own authority when complaining about a mark on an essay or test. "I think that I did a better job on my essay than this mark says I did; I don't think that I deserved such a low mark." I have also heard, "I read Tom's paper; he got a better mark than I did; but I thought my paper was much better than his." Under the weight of such authority one is inclined to say : "My goodness, that's dreadful; I ought to apologize for making you feel so bad; here, let me have your essay; now, what would you like me to put on it?" But such a response would be inadvisable because an instructor would be charged with a *misuse of humor*. Still, with the right gesticulations a genuine smile might be coaxed out. This might not be such a bad thing because all of us could use a bit of lightening up when confronting such matters. But without the nonverbal cues it would likely be perceived as being sarcastic and frivolous. This having been said, it still holds that a student's appeal to himself as his own authority is less than entirely convincing. And that is not because the authority being appealed to may be a little biased or because there may be a slight conflict of interest, but because the teacher-student context would be reversed. Of course under one interpretation it need not be reversed, and I shall say something about that presently, but the problem of context reversal is important enough that we ought to take a moment to examine it.

The assumption under which a student takes a course is that the instructor or a qualified assistant will evaluate the student's work. And the evaluation is most frequently indicated by the instructor or assistant placing a considered grade on the student's work. This is hardly a ground breaking insight. But a slight problem does arise when the student all of a sudden wants to be the final arbiter of his own work. In essence, at the point at which he appeals to himself as the arbiter of the correctness of his grade he becomes his own instructor, or wishes to be so, which naturally makes one wonder why he bothered to enroll in the course in the first place. So, given that the college or university context defines the student as the one who, because of his lack of education, is to be taught and evaluated, and the instructor as the one who, because of his education, is to do the teaching and evaluating, it seems unreasonable to permit the student at the point of his discomfort about his grade to be his own evaluator. Especially so because the student entered into a tacit agreement which acknowledged this contextual arrangement when he signed up for the course – that is, unless I am missing something: perhaps there are no designated teachers anymore; we are all just facilitators of one another's learning. The logic here, though, dictates that there cannot be any students either, much less grades or transcripts with which to impress a prospective employer.

It might be said that we have not placed the most charitable interpretation on the student's apparently self-justifying comments. Perhaps the student merely intended to say that he was unhappy with his mark, that he did not understand the marginal notes on his essay and that he wanted to find out what went wrong. While this could conceivably be true, I do not think that such an interpretation gives enough credit to the student's powers of discrimination. For I have had many students complain in just such an articulate manner; apparently they did not need or want to appeal to their own authority. Nor have the ones who have apparently appealed to their own authority seemed intellectually inferior to the ones who have not. Moreover, it occasionally happens that a student receives an explanation as to what went wrong with his essay, understands it, but remains unhappy with his grade, thinking that he deserved a better one. So, here, as elsewhere, enlightenment does not always guarantee satisfaction (or education, as we saw in Chapter 1).

We freely admit that we have not covered all the possibilities, and this is because often, even in the cases cited here, the complete context is not known. The student may have become less articulate than he was capable of being when he issued his complaint. And the fighter-pilot mother may also have possessed a degree in philosophy. And so forth. On the basis of the contextual information we have, we must make our judgments, while at the same time acknowledging the fact that a fuller contextual account might urge us to alter our thinking sharply.

But whatever the final word on the contextual details may be, it is a safe bet, given our information, that the degree of expertise that the student possesses does not make him a relevant authority which he should quote on his own behalf when complaining about a grade.

But isn't it conceivable that the student is a genius who has written a paper that the instructor just doesn't understand? Conceivable, yes. Likely? No. There are at least two reasons for this being an implausible scenario. First of all, if the paper somehow seemed brilliant but impenetrable, all of the instructors whom I know would invite the student to explain himself before putting a grade on the paper. And second, the assumption about brilliance and impenetrability itself needs to be questioned. It is not a necessary sign of genius that the author's written work be impenetrable. Indeed the contrary is closer to the truth. I am reminded here of a distinction which ought always to be borne in mind when reading anything: obscurity does not imply profundity. It is true that the difficulty of a piece of written work to a significant extent is to be found in the eye of the beholder. And it is also true that some of the great works of philosophy have been written in a turgid style which is close to being impenetrable. But there are at least two conclusions that do not follow from this. From the fact that some of the great works of philosophical literature are stylistically opaque it does not follow that most of them are. And secondly, even if most of them were turgidly written, it does not follow from this that they had to be written in that manner to convey the same message.

Nor is this observation meant to imply that everything that *can* be written can be written so that every literate person can understand it. But it may still be true that whatever *can* be written can be written straightforwardly, even if what is written is very complex and difficult for most people to understand. Given these qualifications, then, is it not conceivable that the student about whom we are speaking, namely Waldo, could have written a very complex work in a straightforward style such as I have just mentioned? It is conceivable that *some* student has done or could do this – but not Waldo. That's because Waldo's fractured grammar and scrambled syntax buried his genius much too deeply for me to be able to unearth it by using the skills required to understand straightforward prose. And this naturally returns us to a point made earlier. Either the impenetrable work will be clearly but complexly written, in which case an instructor will likely ask for clarification, or, what is much more probable, it will be obscurely written usually because of the convoluted grammar or syntax of the essay. To ensure that our discussion of this issue does not drift from its realistic moorings, it needs to be mentioned that even if the first-year student is exceptionally gifted in a subject and has written a complex essay in clear, uncluttered prose, it is again extremely unlikely that it would be so difficult that a Ph.D. in the subject would not be able to understand the essay and credit it for the brilliance it contains.

Let us collect our thoughts. We identified two general concerns pertaining to Waldo's appeal to the authority of his English-teaching mother. The first one had to do with the degree to which the expertise of Waldo's mother is relevant to the complaint he made. And the second one had to do with the question of whether the degree of relevance of the expertise of Waldo's mother should even be considered pertinent to the problem of what to do with Waldo's complaint. Thus far we have dealt only with the first concern, and the conclusion is as follows. It is highly unlikely that Waldo is a misunderstood genius who is justified in appealing to his own authority. And Waldo's appeal to his own authority, given his almost certain lack of expertise, is plainly irrelevant to the proper assessment of his essay grade. Barring expertise of which we are unaware, the fighter-pilot mother may have somewhat more authority than her freshman son even if only because she has completed a university degree. We might further say that the English-teaching mother has more expertise and authority than the fighter-pilot mother because her profession requires her to deal with ideas and attend carefully to the use of language. But none of the "authorities" appealed to in the series has the expertise in dealing with philosophical ideas that the instructor who graded the assignment has. Although the mother who teaches English certainly must deal with ideas, and does have expertise in the use of the English language, both of which are important to the enterprise of teaching and learning philosophy, she will not likely have been forced to analyse rigorously and put into logical form the arguments with which she deals; nor will she likely have been required to teach her students to do so. Nor also will she have been required to deal with the same subject matter in as much depth as the philosophy instructor has been required to do.[1]

But what if a student should appeal to a relevant or even highly relevant authority? What if he should appeal, as I have heard students do several times, to a friend who is a fourth year honours student in philosophy; or better yet, which I have rarely heard done, what if he should appeal to another philosophy instructor who teaches nearly the same course and who, let us suppose, thinks that the essay is good? Although one could still cogently argue that the fourth year honors student's expertise and familiarity with the course material and assignment are still no match for those of the instructor, one would be hard pressed to argue convincingly for the same conclusion when considering the expertise of the outside instructor. This now takes us to the more important of our concerns in dealing with student appeals to outside "authorities."

Perhaps the reason that I have rarely heard of such an appeal to an outside instructor is partly because most students would not be closely enough acquainted with another instructor to approach him or her about such a matter, or because they would be uneasy about taking a paper from the instructor who graded it to another instructor in order to get a more positive opinion on the work. This leads us directly to the other, larger part of the answer. Most of the instructors whom I know would not even read, or at least would not evaluate, a student's paper which a colleague had already graded. The reason for this may be given in a single word: "professionalism." Not only are instructors conscious of its implications, but so too are many students. By looking at the connotation of this word we can begin to answer our question concerning the relevance of outside authorities to the matter of student appeals for higher grades.

"Professionalism" is defined as follows: "the methods, manner or spirit of a profession" (Funk & Wagnalls). The unspecified connotations that have been given to the meaning of the word by professional groups, including college instructors, help us to unpack the contents of words like "manner" and "spirit." Part of what is included in a professional manner or spirit is a discreteness of behavior which one member of the profession shows towards other members. And the specific meaning of this discrete-behavior will vary with the professions being considered. But whatever behaviors are considered to be indiscrete within the profession, the negative evaluation of them is usually made to preserve the autonomy which certified members of that profession have earned. In the case of college and university instructors specifically this means that when a judgment is made by a member of the profession about the work of a student being taught by that member, then it is indiscrete for another member of the profession deliberately to pass judgment on the former member's judgment. This is because it would interfere with the freedom of independent judgment which the instructor has earned by meeting the rigorous formal qualifications of his profession. Often these are the highest standards of certification which the profession has set. Is there anything other than professional discretion to justify the belief that one instructor normally ought not to evaluate a grade given to a student by another instructor or who is in charge of the student's course? Yes, I think there is. And the key is found in the phrase "normally ought not to evaluate."

First of all there is no need to lapse into naivete when considering this delicate subject of instructors and their assumed right to evaluate autonomously their students. Physicians sometimes disagree in their diagnoses of a condition which a patient may have. Moreover, they often disagree radically about whether alternative forms of therapy should be administered; to mention only a few: certain kinds of diet therapy, sublingual testing, acupuncture and chiropractic. Supreme court judges often disagree in their judgments and consequently reach resolution only by a *majority* decision. Moreover, scientists frequently differ, not merely in their theorizing but also in their interpretation of data; and not just in the "soft" sciences, but in the "hard" sciences as well. It should come as no surprise therefore to hear that philosophers differ in their opinions about all sorts of matters. In short, the experts in every field differ. But from this it does not follow that they differ about everything, all the time. There is much about which they do agree and this is often found at the rudimentary level of the discipline, at the alphabet stage so to speak (though admittedly, even here they sometimes disagree). And believe it or not, while philosophy instructors might disagree about whether a student should receive a 5 or a 6 on an essay, there would be very few, if any, cases where one instructor would award a grade of 4 on an essay, when another instructor with equal qualifications would award a 9. The point still remains, that the experts can and do differ. Then does this not justify a student's going from one expert to another until he finds satisfaction? And should not this information be taken back to the original expert whose judgment produced the initial dissatisfaction?

No, I do not think that this is what the fact of disagreement among the experts teaches us. For that fact should not be inspected in isolation from other essential facts. To take the supreme court example, a decision on a case must be reached and the decision must be final. These are both practical matters. Questioning and musing about a murder case, for instance, cannot go on forever, especially since the person whose life is being weighed in the balance of justice may be languishing in prison. Sad as it undoubtedly is, we have only so much time in which to get a multitude of goals accomplished, and we find that our life-span is all too finite. This fact applies directly to the question of the student who appeals to an outside authority to get the satisfaction regarding his grade that he desires. It is simply not practical for an instructor to take to heart the negative evaluations that his students convey from English-teaching mothers, or even from outside instructors at the University of Complete Knowledge, if that is what the complaint should amount to. One could apply a *reductio ad absurdum* argument to this problem by asking himself what would be the case if we did not take time constraints seriously.

Suppose that Waldo brings a critical note regarding his grade from his English-teaching mother to his philosophy instructor. The philosophy instructor takes to heart the contents of the note and phones the mother. After a spirited discussion with the instructor, the mother realizes that her opinion has really had quite an effect. She is not convinced by the instructor's justification for the grade he put on her son's paper, and she phones around the University of Complete Knowledge until she finds a sympathetic ear. Luckily, the Ear is a philosophical one and is only too happy to take up the mother's cause. The Ear then phones the less-than-completely-knowledgeable instructor who started this business by putting the unwelcome grade on Waldo's paper. Now the two instructors of philosophy are at it. The issue is not resolved by the phone conversation and the Ear marshals support from his colleagues at UCK. Realizing that his reputation is on the line, the unkindly grading instructor starts to marshall his own support by phoning some international authorities who may lend him their support. By now the Fax machines are humming and all parties are consuming generous quantities of alcohol and eating unprecedented numbers of antacid tablets. That is, all parties except Waldo, who is enjoying the fray immensely, and whose major concern in life has shifted slightly, from the injustice of receiving a low grade to increasing his eye-hand co-ordination in order to be able to rescue the princess in the computer game *Prince of Persia*. Bear in mind that the disputation began in early October; it is now the middle of December; the final exam has been written and the instructor cannot give Waldo a final grade. And when he will be able to do so remains a mystery.

To try to ensure that the wrong impression is not given to this account of a student appealing to an outside authority, I have been at pains to say that the discussion applies in "normal" circumstances. I would be quite unhappy if it were concluded that I do not think that students should have an opportunity to appeal their grades. The appeals we have been talking about are informal in nature, in which a student comes to his instructor's office to complain about a low grade, and in the process refers to an outside "authority," for example, his mother, to change the instructor's thinking about the grade he put on the essay. Clearly students should have the right to appeal their grades. They ought to exercise that right if the normal practice of consulting their instructor about the details of their grades has been followed and they still sincerely think they have not been treated fairly. In the vast majority of cases the marginal comments which an instructor puts on a paper or test are sufficient to explain to the student why he received the grade he did. And in most of the cases that remain, in which the marginal comments have not satisfactorily explained the reason for the grade, almost always the questions are answered satisfactorily by an instructor during office hours. But occasionally, even after sincere attempts have been made by the instructor to explain the rationale for the grade and sincere attempts have been made by the student to understand the rationale, communication breaks down. I have used the word "sincere" advisedly, because without good will on the part of both parties even the need for the very few cases that go to formal arbitration is thrown into question.

Most institutions have formal appeal procedures in place; and they should do so because all of us ought be accountable for the jobs we are paid to do. A student is advised to seek clarification from his instructor if the marginal comments on his assignment do not make it clear why he received the grade he did. And the instructor ought to be able to provide such a clarification. Resolution of course implies not only the sincerity which was mentioned above but also a comprehension by the student of the explanations which the instructor has given. But granting that sincerity and comprehension are both present, and the student still thinks that justice has not been done, he ought to appeal formally his grade.

All the formal appeal policies which I have read contain fairly strict procedures which the student and his institution must follow. For example, the formal appeal must be made in writing by the student within a specified period of time after his grade has been received. And there is usually more than one level of authority beyond that of the student's instructor through which his formal appeal may proceed. If he is not satisfied with the decision reached after his complaint has been heard at the first level, then he may proceed with his complaint to a higher level. (Institutions vary on the number and kinds of authority which exist on the hierarchy of levels of appeal, so students are advised to familiarize themselves with the procedures which pertain to their institution.) But we must not lose sight of the main point of our investigation of the student's appeal to an outside authority.

Even though there are multiple levels of authority in the formal process, the process itself must come to a stop at the highest level of authority to which the appeal can be made. And this need for termination is no different in the formal process than it is in the informal process. Practicality, which largely means the need to limit the time spent on the process, dictates that there be a final appeal and a final judgment. So, even if the institution should consult outside philosophical authorities to adjudicate the merit of Waldo's essay, the process of consultation cannot go on indefinitely. Indeed, for the practical reasons already stated, the institution usually tries to conclude a formal appeal as soon as possible, not the least reason for which is the need the registrar has to complete the student's transcript.

To summarize then, when a student informally appeals to an outside authority while complaining to his instructor about the grade he received on an assignment, the instructor will not likely take his appeal seriously, for two good reasons.[2] First, the authority is nearly always either an irrelevant authority or a not-relevant-enough authority for the professor to give the appeal serious attention. This precisely means that the expertise and experience of an outside authority, as well as the authority's familiarity with the course work within which the grade was given, are almost always much less than those of the instructor who awarded the grade, if not absent altogether. Through many years of study and testing the instructor has qualified himself in his profession and has earned the right to make autonomous judgments about the value of his student's work.

But more importantly, the instructor must take his own judgment to be final at the informal level for the practical reason that, if he did not do this, he would undoubtedly find himself embroiled in far flung discussions which would drain his energies and reduce his effectiveness in the course. Moreover, if he did not do this, his actions could easily turn out to be a disbenefit to the student, because eventually his wide-ranging discussions could prevent the student from actually completing his course of study and moving forward in his educational development when he wants to.

If after making a sincere attempt to get the explanation for his unsatisfactory grade from his instructor or in the informal setting of an office discussion, the student still thinks he has been treated unfairly, then he has recourse to the formal appeal procedures of his institution. However, along this formal route he will find that his appeal to authority must also come to a stop at a practically specified level, just as it did along the informal route.

3

Complaints About Exams, Tests, and Classmarks

5. "How could anyone fail a philosophy course?"

This was the first question which one student who had failed his social ethics course asked me when he entered my office to inquire about his performance on the final exam. But I'm sure that the same preconception also exists in the minds of some students who take other liberal arts subjects: English, for example. For some reason, the notion that a particular academic subject is or should be unfailable lodges deep within the minds of some students, and remains there even in the face of overwhelming evidence to the contrary.

To the question, "How could anyone fail this course?" an instructor is tempted to reply, "You've demonstrated that admirably." This answer, while being to the point perhaps does not quite address the deep puzzlement which the student feels.

Part of the difficulty I believe stems from an entrenched popular conception of the subject which is extremely difficult to dislodge. Students see listed in the college calendar an elective such as Social Ethics and they immediately think, "Oh good, I can talk about that!" They assume that the course will consist of, or at least *should* consist of, a bunch of friendly people sitting around a classroom, each with a nice cup of coffee and a glazed doughnut, "chewing the fat" about trendy issues such as abortion and euthanasia. Attending this image is the belief that everyone's ideas are as good as everyone else's. It therefore comes as a rude awakening to some students that the study of ethics involves learning to analyse, enunciate and remember ethical principles, without which ethical judgments simply cannot be made. It is definitely not comforting for other students to hear that their premises ought to be supported by evidence and that their conclusions should follow logically from their premises. Further to this, it comes as a revelation to many that a student who puts forth an argument whose premises are true and whose conclusion is logically drawn really does have a better argument than another

41

student whose premises and conclusion lack these qualities – and the results of both can be graded according to a set of clearly stated criteria.

I expect that when most instructors of social ethics cover the topic of abortion they will discuss the question of the personhood of the fetus. In doing so, they will most likely want their students to be familiar with at least the species criterion, the potentiality criterion and the actual possession criterion of personhood, together with the objections that have been raised against the use of each criterion. The instructor may wish to go further and raise counter-objections to some of the criteria, and even pose objections to the counter-objections. If on his examination the instructor asks a question on the personhood of the fetus, he may very likely expect, and will probably state, that the student demonstrate a facility in dealing with the criteria according to which the personhood issue is decided. Specifically, in this case the instructor will want to see if the student

1. has understood the criteria,
2. has understood the objections, and
3. can write about both in a clear and coherent fashion. There may well be an evaluative component to the question, but this can not usually be addressed in isolation from the descriptive and analytical parts of the answer. Many students seem to think that the evaluative part can be answered satisfactorily without any reference to the detail of specific arguments already discussed in the literature. And this is thought to be so even after such material has been gone over in class, with parts of it being emphasized. As a result, an instructor gets something like "I feel that the fetus is/is not a person . . ." without any reference to arguments which have grappled with this question.

So, the simple answer to the question "how could anyone fail this course?" is: by not satisfactorily answering the questions. One can fail to answer satisfactorily the question by neglecting to learn the specific details of a complete answer to the questions; and before that, by dismissing the fact that there are criteria or standards for good answers in philosophy no less than there are standards for good answers in physics or mathematics. [See Chapter 1, endnote 8.]

Still, after all of this has been said – and likely it *was* said in class more than once – there will still be a few who cling to the warm and fuzzy notion that what the course should be about is offering opinions from the wealth of one's unreflective experience, or, in other words, "shooting the breeze." But when the idea of learning the "discipline" is rejected outright, not much can be done to convince someone to look for those standards which an academic subject invariably has, much less convince him to meet the standards.

6. "But I thought I understood the material."

Several years ago a student named Susan asked me why she was making such low marks in my course. First I asked her if she had understood my lectures as well as the ideas which were being debated in the class discussions. She said that she did. I had no reason to doubt her word, especially since she had shown an understanding of some of the material by her perceptive comments in class.

More recently another student, Richard, came into my office after receiving the unexpected news that he had failed my course. He said, "I don't see how I could have failed, because I read the text over three times and I thought I understood the material." I have no doubt that he was sincere. But I am equally confident that there are some truths about the activities of learning, reproducing what one has learned, and applying what one has learned, of which both Susan and Richard were unaware.

However, before we look at these activities it is important to mention the most obvious possibility. Richard may have been sincere, but also he may have been sincerely mistaken in his assessment of his own understanding of the material. It is quite possible that either he did not understand what he thought he understood or he did not understand it as well as he thought he did. In both cases an instructor or a test or both are needed to reveal and correct the discrepancy which exists between what the student believes he understands and what he actually does understand. The words of Robert Burns come to mind: "O wad some Pow'r the giftie gie us / To see oursels as others see us!"[1] I shall say something more about this at the end of this section, but let us assume for the moment that the student's understanding and his ability to understand are not in question.

Almost all of us have had the experience of sitting in a high school math class listening to the teacher explain a proof. For me it was a geometry class. My friends and I understood the concepts that the teacher was developing on the chalk board and we left the the class feeling quite confident that we knew what was going on. Consequently we felt no need to go over the material at home or to work out the problems in the text which required that we apply the ideas in the geometry proof in creative ways. Then came the shock. We arrived at the examination and read the question that required a detailed knowledge of the proof and realized that we were not really familiar with it. In short, we did not know what we previously knew, or thought we knew. What happened in the interim, between the teacher's going over the proof and our staring dumbly at that examination question which required us to handle the concepts of the proof in an intimate fashion?

First, we did not realize that there is a huge difference between being able to follow the teacher's explanation one day in class and being able to reproduce that explanation at a later date outside class. And this is true whether we are trying to reproduce the proof in the teacher's words or in our own. Understanding a proof or a concept is admittedly the important first step to learning it well enough to reproduce it on an examination – but it is only the first step. What is also needed is the process of going over the proof enough times until we can remember the steps sufficiently well to tell them to someone else, either orally or on paper. In brief, we first need to understand the concept, then to go over the concept enough times to remember it and reproduce it.

Beyond this, there is an important stage which can be reached only by working with the proof in novel ways, applying its main insights to problems not encountered before. By this means the main ideas are assimilated into our system of thinking. This holds true not only for math proofs but also for most other disciplines as well; and this especially includes philosophy whose abstract ideas can easily slip away from us if we do not go over them in our minds and apply them. Therefore, it is important to practise enunciating the ideas and to use them in discussion so that they will become embedded in our thinking.

A more complicated story about mastering academic material no doubt can be written. My purpose here, however, is to identify just the main outlines of the story so that the sincere student who wants to know why he failed or made a low grade may do so rather quickly. The basic answer is this: the student may well have understood the material, but perhaps did not remember it; or he may have remembered it but did not know how to apply it in a novel way on the examination.

Consider the course in which the student may be required to demonstrate an understanding of the distinction between Voluntary Active Euthanasia (VAE) and Voluntary Passive Euthanasia (VPE). He must first learn the definitions. "VAE is the act of killing someone who is going to die soon anyway, at the person's own request, as an act of kindness"; and "VPE is the act of letting someone die who is going to die soon anyway, as an act of kindness."[2] This alone is a significant enough task, but an instructor may require more on the examination. He may require the student to apply his knowledge of the definition in a novel situation. For example the instructor may ask the following question "If in the case of VAE, the patient says "kill me" and the physician says "I will kill you," what do the patient and physician say in the case of VPE?

Given such a question a student may be able to remember the definitions of VAE and VPE but may not see clearly the essential distinction between the two. He must have thought about, or be able to think on the spot about the difference between killing and letting die, and to see how this distinction is manifested in the language of both the patient and the physician. Putting oneself successively in their shoes will help to secure the answer.

It is possible that occasionally a student will encounter a subject for which his natural gifts do not especially suit him. Possibly this was Richard's basic problem. The kind of mind which the student has may not be suited to dealing successfully with philosophical concepts, which often require the use of both analytical thinking and imagination. Although the idea that one needs a modicum of talent to succeed in a discipline is not a popular idea, it is nonetheless true. So another possible reason for the persistent difference between a student's expectations and performance is simply the fact that his expectations are unrealistically high.

Now, a different but equally important truth about succeeding in any course ought to be registered. Self-confidence and determination will often carry a student to levels of achievement which otherwise he would not attain. And I do not wish in anything I say to undermine these important qualities. Therefore, the realization of there being a possible discrepancy between expectation and performance needs to be balanced with the realization that one should not give in to the discouragement which often follows the news of a failing grade. It may be appropriate for the student to say something like "I will pass it the next time" and to work doggedly toward the realization of that goal. For surely one of the chief causes of under-achievement is lack of effort.

We can summarize by saying that a student who sincerely thinks he should be making higher grades may not be doing so for one or more of the following reasons:

1. he may not understand the material because
   (i) he needs more time to grasp the material, or
   (ii) his gifts do not particularly equip him to grasp the material;
2. he may have understood the material but not remembered it; that is, he may not have gone over it enough times to reproduce it;
3. he may have understood the material and remembered it, but not have mastered it; that is, he may not have appropriated the ideas to his own thinking, by extracting the main ideas and applying them correctly in novel situations.

7. "You took away four of my marks because I'm a quiet person."

To understand properly this student's complaint, the reader needs to be acquainted with the context within which the complaint was made.

In nearly all my courses I give 10-15 percent of the final grade for class participation. Every semester, at the beginning of each course I explain
1. why I have a classmark,
2. how it will be calculated, and
3. how a student can earn a good classmark.

Let me deal with these in turn.

It is my assumption that the scheduling of classes at colleges and universities is for some good purpose. Presumably there are good reasons for an instructor to show up for classes and for students to attend the lectures. If there aren't such good reasons, then scandalously we are wasting huge amounts of time and money. But I believe that there are such good reasons.

The value of attending class regularly can be seen by considering the learning experiences that are missed by the solitary student who seldom attends class.

First, if the textual material contains many difficult concepts, the solitary student will miss the instructor's explanations of much of the course content. But even if the textual material is manageable without the aid of an instructor, the student will miss the extra-textual material which instructors frequently include in their lectures.

Equally important, the student misses out on the frequent dialogical exchange which takes place in a class, or at least which should do so. This is especially noticeable in a subject like philosophy or English (though I believe the same argument holds to an equal or lesser degree for practically all other disciplines as well). Assuming a small class of forty or less, a student may enter into a dialogical exchange with his classmates as well as his instructor. He has the advantage not only of asking questions of clarification and exploration but also of hearing others do the same.[3]

Given the value of the instructor's explanations of difficult work in class and the value of the many types of dialogical exchange which result from hearing the work explained, amplified, augmented and applied to questions raised in class, is it fair to give the student who rarely attends class the same grade, other things being equal, as the one who never misses class? Is it fair to give the student who almost always shows up for class and whose regular and informed participation makes for a stimulating learning environment for all the students, the same reward as the student who rarely attends class – namely, nothing?

So, for these reasons, among others, I take it that it is important to a student's education that he attend lectures regularly. If it truly is important, and I believe it is, then credit should be given for attending class and participating in discussion; and accordingly, a lack of credit for failure to do so. But to give such credit on the basis of something more than the vague memory of who was present and when, it is important to have as accurate a record as possible of each student's presence in class. Hence, I am probably one of the three remaining instructors in the Western World who takes attendance in his university courses. I have used two methods in the past: one is to draw up a seating plan in which students who wish to, have the option of choosing their own seats; the other is to pass around a class list on which students can write their initials in the column under the date for that day's lecture. A classmark of 10 percent is made up of two parts: 5 percent is given for attendance and 5 percent for class participation. A high class mark can be earned by regular and informed participation in class. It goes (almost) without saying that a student cannot regularly participate in class unless he or she regularly attends class; nor can a student participate in an informed way unless he or she studies the assigned readings from the texts in preparation for the class meeting. Here I am reminded of an adage used by a former classics professor of mine: "Even a fool can ask a question that a wise man can't answer." An example would be, "What does it all mean?"

To summarize, then, 5 easy points can be earned by attending all the lectures and 5 points can be earned through informed participation in class in the various ways suggested by my comments above. I say other things about the classmark as well, explaining in more detail how each of the 5 points is calculated; but perhaps enough has been said already to appreciate the student complaint with which we started, and to which we now return.[4] Given the context which I have just sketched, what ought one to say to Brent when he complains about getting 6 out of 10 for a classmark: "You took away four of my marks because I am a quiet student"?

First of all, Brent did not have any marks to begin with; so none could have been taken away. It was his responsibility to *earn* a higher mark by fulfilling the requirements for a good classmark mentioned above. So the blame cannot rightly be placed at the instructor's door: it belongs to Brent.

Concerning the matter of Brent being a quiet student, a number of things need to be said. First, Brent "knew the score" at the beginning of the course. Presumably he knew then that he was a quiet student. Supposing he had a choice, why didn't he simply drop the course and choose another? Did he hope unrealistically that even if he remained silent in class all semester he would receive the same classmark as the student who contributed questions, criticisms and exploratory ideas frequently? To credit Brent with the same classmark as the one given to Ruth, who was a regular contributor to class discussions, would be unfair. While Brent was listening, Ruth was working much harder, to engage her instructor or classmates in the process of intellectual discovery.

As it so happens, Ruth is not an especially extroverted student either; but she worked hard, kept up on the class readings and *extended* herself while in class. Ruth is not by any means a rare student. She is among the many who realize that although their personalities incline them to behave in one direction, they must work at extending themselves in the opposite direction if they wish to succeed. This general principle needs to be grasped by more students. And they need to be assured that for very many good students, not everything that they do well comes easily to them. Indeed, their success is bought with a great deal of effort, self-denial and often pain.

8. "But I made a 9 in psychology!"[5]

This was a comment made by a student who visited my office to find out why she did so poorly on her philosophy test. I am given to understand by my colleagues that comments like this one are fairly common. They are certainly common in my teaching experience. In the complaint above one may substitute for the discipline of psychology practically any other discipline one likes, such as mathematics, history or Greek, and get the same message.

This complaint is symptomatic of a misunderstanding that exists in the minds of many students who enter college or university. Somehow the idea has lodged in their thinking that if they work for X hours on subject A and score 75 percent, then by working X hours on any other subject, B or C or D, then they should be able to score at least 75 percent on any of those subjects as well. A corollary to this is that if they can score 40 percent by working X hours on A, then they should be able to score 80 percent by working 2X hours on A.

Considering the corollary first, it is unfortunate that getting good grades doesn't work like that. The relationship between the time a student studies and the mark she makes is more likely to be an exponential relationship than a linear one. That is to say, whereas she may be able to earn a passing or near-passing grade with little study, she may have to spend a disproportionately larger amount of time studying to earn a distinguished grade. For instance, although it may take only one hour per week to make a mark of 40 percent on a particular subject, it may well take eight hours per week for the same student to make 80 percent in the same subject. And since the amount of disproportionate work will vary with the student involved, it is quite possible (because it does happen) that some students will never be able to earn 80 percent in the subject, no matter how many hours per week they devote to the subject.

This last observation brings to our attention something that seems to be minimized these days in primary and secondary schools, if it is talked about at all: namely, that people not only have markedly different talents, but also have them to markedly different degrees. If this quite obvious truth is not permitted to register in the minds of students before they enter college or university, then they will approach their university courses with false expectations, and these are bound to cause them disappointment and even grief. An effective way of suppressing the truth about variations and degrees of talent among students is for the primary and secondary school system to permit all students to pass through the system ungraded, and thus to go through school without any possibility of failing. To put the matter another way, the student is conditioned to expect that he will make the grade without satisfying the requisite standard. He grows up almost unable to see the correspondence between talent and work on the one hand and academic standing on the other. Over many years he has been coached to expect good results irrespective of the native talent he may possess and of how he uses that talent. It may make the little ones feel cozier at first, but when the little ones become big ones, while still retaining their infantile attachment to the notion that all students should do equally well in every subject, if only they try equally hard, they will experience confusion, frustration and anxiety. This confusion is manifested in such comments as, "but I don't understand why I did so poorly in your course: I made a 9 in psychology!"

One of the ways by which to make students aware of the differences in ability among them, without all of a sudden discouraging them, is to deal with the matter of expectations at the beginning of the semester. Often I ask students to tell me with a show of hands if they have had difficulty with mathematics in high school. Since more students seem to find difficulty with math than with any other subject, I usually get a good number of hands shooting up. I then use this demonstration to explain what should be an obvious truth: that if many students found, after working diligently, that they did poorly in math, or at least poorer than they had hoped to do, they should not find it strange to suppose that some students may not do pleasingly well in philosophy, or indeed in any subject which requires them to deal with abstract ideas.

I should mention that I do not leave the matter there, but go on to talk about the real value of exposing oneself to the discipline of an unfamiliar subject, even if one can not master the discipline or do as well in it as one might like. Here we need to be wary of a rationalization in which students and others alike unfortunately take comfort: "If I can't be good at it, it can't be good." For in such rationalizations lie the impediments to our self-improvement.

The student who says, "all my other grades are 8s and 9s" is not saying anything which must reveal a contradiction, or even anything unusual about his situation. Assuming that the student worked as hard on the questionable subject as he did on the ones that brought him 8s and 9s, the reasons are likely to be quite straightforward. Perhaps the unrewarding subject is more demanding than any of the others, or perhaps the student is not as talented in that subject as in the others, or quite possibly both together are true. These don't exhaust the possible answers to the student's question, but most of the remaining ones probably don't require us to look for any sort of oddness in the situation about which we ought to be fretful.[6]

4

More Irrelevant Complaints

9. "I need an 8 to get into law school." or "My problem is your problem."[1]

Whether or not student attitudes toward getting good grades have changed on a large scale, I simply cannot say. But I can say that I have noticed in my own teaching that increasingly over the past seven years students have come to my office begging for grades. And this is the experience of many of my colleagues at both colleges and universities elsewhere. Begging comes in various forms and has occurred in my office numerous times; but on two occasions the students were notably aggressive in making their needs known to me. One student said, "I *need* an 8 to get into Law School" and she repeated it with emphasis, as though to say, "Do you hear me, I *need* an 8." Another student who was failing the course and freely admitted that she did not understand much of what was being said in class or in the text, said repeatedly, "I need a 4 in this course. I simply can't fail this course." This was said with an inflection that is difficult to capture on paper, but the essence of it was this: "Look Santa Claus, I've been a good girl, so you'd better deliver on that bike; because if you don't, I'm not going to be able to go riding with my friends – I'll really look stupid, and it will be all your fault, and your reputation as a nice guy is going to be shot!"

I was visited by another student named Lance who played football and whose imposing presence is memorable. His height when he was sitting down seemed equal to mine when I was standing up; and his physique, at an estimated 250 lbs., made my frame look like a neglected chain-store mannequin. Putting his case with all the delicacy for which his training had equipped him, he said: "I didn't take this course to fail it!" Despite the strident tone, I had to agree. What he said was most likely true, even if not enlightening.

Not all grade begging is aggressive. Sometimes it is done with a pleasant smile in a most congenial tone. "All my life I've wanted to be a brain surgeon. It sure would be nice if I could pass this course and fulfill my life-long dream."

What should an instructor say in such cases? Several answers seem appropriate. In all of them, however, it is important for the student to see the illogical nature of his request; and to see that he is trying to rid himself of his problem by making somebody else responsible for it. What he is basically saying is this: "my problem is your problem." To begin with, then, the instructor should kindly but firmly say: "that's *your* problem, not mine." The student needs to see that his not being able to get into a future program because of a present grade is squarely his responsibility. It is his job to satisfy the criteria which the instructor has set for achieving good grades in the course and therefore for earning the grade required for entrance into the desired future program. It is not the instructor's responsibility to ensure that the student gets the grade he needs in order to make it to the next step in his imagined program of automatic success. While all of this may seem painfully obvious to the reader, many students don't seem to have grasped this idea: if they had worked harder, they might well have earned the grade they desired; getting the desired grade was, and is, *their* responsibility.

There is an important ethical dimension to this matter of begging for grades of which the student ought to be made aware. If an instructor were to heed the pleas for unearned grades she would not only be granting the begging student a grade he did not deserve, but she would also be putting the student's classmates at an unfair disadvantage.[2]

The other students do not have an equal opportunity to tell their "hard luck stories" and to impress upon their instructor how much they really *need* to have the grade they want. Apart from the moral question of giving unearned grades upon request, imagine the logistical difficulty of having all the students file in to the instructor's office after every final exam to tell her about their pressing needs. In addition, acceding to the request of the begging student would send a clear negative signal to him about the value of work and achievement, which itself would be unfair; for the work-a-day world into which he will likely migrate is not likely to be in the least forgiving.[3]

In summary, then, capitulating to the practice of begging for grades promotes two kinds of unfairness:
1. it is unfair to the student to give him a grade he did not earn, and
2. it is unfair to the student's classmates.

The obviousness of the irrationality of begging for grades makes one wonder where the students who practise it have got the idea. Why do they think that it is their desires and not their earning power which should predominate in the business of getting good grades? Are they being taught by word or example, at home or at school, that no one should be permitted to earn less than he hopes to earn at academic work? Whatever its origin, such an attitude, if not soundly checked, will result in an increasing number of people, even so-called educated people, going out into our society expecting to get for nothing those things which must be earned. How can they help but expect handouts in those very areas where the point of the employment is to do an honest day's work for an agreed upon wage? Imagine the absurdity of a newly hired employee who receives his first pay cheque and confronts his boss: "Yes, I read the contract and I know the salary scale; but you see, I really need more money to buy the house of my dreams; so, will you please give me more money."

10. "My primary school teachers discovered that I was gifted."

The context of this comment was a visit which a student had made to my office, ostensibly to learn why he had made such a low mark on his assignment. But the subtext seemed to read as follows: "I'm really a very bright guy; someone with my intelligence shouldn't be receiving poor marks like this. They don't fit very well with my potential." Beyond this point the guesswork becomes less reliable; but perhaps the student also meant to suggest that because he was so bright I should either have changed his mark or at least be prepared to keep his luminosity before me when I graded his next assignment.

Such unbiased personal comments made by students about their own cleverness are not unusual in my experience: I get at least two of such comments every year. My opening response is the same in each case: *"No one gets paid for sitting around being capable of doing something."*[4]

And this obtains whether the payment is being made in dollars or in grades. Simply stated, potential is not enough. The ability to perform an academic task will not, by itself, get the task accomplished, much less accomplished well. Although this too is a truism, it seems to be unknown to some students, especially some of the bright ones.

There is another dimension to this problem which is worth considering. When I hear students extolling their own abilities I often wonder if the self-congratulation is being used as a buffer against anticipated failure. The question takes me back to my own early schooling, to somewhere around the seventh grade. Ruby was the "smartest student in the class." At least that was what most people said about her. But smartest or not, there was no doubt about her academic standing. She was at the top of our class in practically every subject. Some of us guys used to make a fetish of not studying for tests and exams. The unspoken rule was, "get as high a mark as you can with as little work as possible." Just before an exam we would try to outdo one another with feats of lethargy. And of course on exam day the guy who left the examination room first got an extra portion of admiration from the rest of us. If he could "finish" the exam in half the allotted time, well, then, there was no limit to the respect in which he could hope to bask. Of course the inverted snobbery did not stop there. We would compare grades after we got our exams back and the bragging would start up again. Comments like this were common: "I made 72, but I spent only a half hour looking over my notes the night before – Ruby, she studies four hours a night. If I studied that much I could make 98 too!" Someone else, ready to outdo the others, would chime in with "Half an hour!? I didn't crack a book and I got 68!"

Although we were quite unaware of the exponential rule for getting good grades which I outlined in case study no. 8, upon looking back I am now convinced that the root of our problem was to be found elsewhere. It now seems to me that we were basically afraid of something. We were afraid that if we tried our best we might not *be* the best in the class. If we studied Ruby's four hours every night, we might not make Ruby's 98s. Bright as we thought we were, maybe we weren't as bright as Ruby. As long as we didn't *apply* our ability we didn't have to face any unpleasantness about our standing; and we could always soothe our egos with comforting words about how much we could really do if we wanted to try. But why didn't we want to try? Ah, there's the rub.[5] Let's face it: there are many bright students at college and university, some brighter than others. Is the "gifted" student in some cases not living up to his or her potential because of a fear of falling short of his or her expectations? And is much of the student's self-congratulation about his own brightness, together with his lack of sincere hard work, a means of guarding against anticipated failure or an anticipated shortfall in his performance? A more searching question than these is the question of how students come to think this way. Surely the answer, to speak generally, is not to do away with grades, hoping in that way to avoid bruising anyone's ego. Rather, it is to emphasize the value of doing one's best in order to fulfill one's potential, to exhaust oneself, so to speak, in order to be able to know oneself better and thus more effectively to direct one's energies in the pursuit of life's important goals.

If talent and hard work are each necessary conditions for getting good grades at university, are they jointly sufficient conditions? It would be pleasant to be able to answer this question with an unqualified Yes. Unfortunately, such an easy answer would neglect other necessary conditions to which we must now turn our attention.

We have not said what we mean by "good grades." And it is true that not all bright and diligent students will consider the same range of grades to be good. This is partly because some bright and diligent students are brighter and more diligent than others. But it is also because students who are equally capable and hard working have different expectations of themselves. Let us assume then that we are dealing with students who are roughly equal in their abilities, expectations and commitment to hard work. Even among this class of students some will be found who have not learned how to apply their abilities efficiently. Such students do not lack ability: they lack the skills needed to make the best use of their ability.

In the world of business people talk about "working smarter" instead of "working harder" to get the same amount of work done. The idea here is to make efficient use of one's time: for example, to have a time set aside to open the mail, instead of interrupting oneself every time a letter or parcel comes dribbling into the office; to handle each piece of paper only once before doing something constructive with it; blocking off the most productive times of the day for work on company projects that need a creative touch; and so on. In a similar vein, thoughtfully scheduling one's study time and learning efficient study habits will enable students to gain a maximum benefit from a certain limited amount of time available to them outside classes. Then, too, every liberal arts student needs to know how most effectively to attack an essay assignment. Effectively managing one's time and writing clear, concise and systematic essays are skills which *can* be learned. Even the brightest student may need to avail himself of the remedial opportunities that his institution provides in order to do his best and to get those "good grades" he desires. Sadly, it is possible to be both bright and hard-working, yet to spend 25 inefficient hours on an essay, for the most part intellectually thrashing about in an aimless manner.

The first action for such a student to take, then, is to check with the student services division of his institution to see what skill-building seminars are offered on his campus. In the event that no such services are available, a student can be encouraged to consult books in the library which address the problem of becoming efficient at doing good academic work.[6]

11. "I have three part-time jobs."

About two years ago Paul came to my office looking quite dejected. He had just received the results of his first philosophy test and they were not promising. A bare pass, understandably, was not his idea of academic success, and he was already starting to worry about failing the course. I went over his test with him to explain where he had gone wrong, and then listened to him comment on his financial situation and home life.

I soon learned that Paul had been working at, not one, but three part-time jobs; that he was doing his best to support his three children; and that on top of all this he was carrying a full academic load – five courses! He went on to say that he desperately wanted to pass the course and that if he did not pass he would be letting his family down: both by using tuition money which could have gone to meet more immediate needs at home, and because his family was counting on him to get a degree, which would assure them of a better standard of living. Then he asked me what I thought his chances were of passing the course.

I do not believe that an instructor has no responsibility to listen to such hard-luck stories. At the same time, I also believe that an instructor would be acting irresponsibly if he were to allow such stories to influence him when grading the work of needful students like Paul. Among the other things wrong with such an emotional response would be the unfairness it would show to all those students who did not have a chance to speak with their instructor and make what might well turn out to be an equally touching appeal. They, too, might expect that their appeal would mitigate the dismal results of their impending examination, which might, for whatever reason, be only half-heartedly done. There is another more obvious reason, though, for not allowing such hard-luck stories to influence one's judgment when grading papers, and I shall attend to that reason presently. But before going too far down that road we need to stop and clarify what has just been said.

I have implied by what I have said that Paul was *appealing to my emotions,* particularly *pity,* and subtly trying to secure a commitment from me that in the end he would pass the course. By my lights the evidence supported this conclusion. As I saw the situation, the evidence was constituted not only by *what* he said, although that alone seemed troubling enough, but also by how he said it, as well as by the placement of what he said within the larger context of the conversation that came before and after. Given all those factors, the complete details of which are not easy to relate on paper, I came to my conclusion about Paul. Although that is what I thought about Paul's intentions, and still think about them, I could have been mistaken in my judgment.[7]

But even if I am not mistaken about Paul it should not be concluded from this complaint alone that all students who tell their troubles to their instructors are looking for special consideration when the final grading time comes. I can recall meetings with several students who did not eagerly tell me about their unfortunate circumstances, but only related them because I had naively asked a question or made a comment whose proper response required that they tell me. But their accounts were usually general and related in a somewhat reluctant manner. For instance, I learned that one student, Cynthia, was clinically depressed, but just during *some* of the academic year. This was revealed only because I had seen a discrepancy between her excellent work in class and on her essays, on the one hand, and her poor performance on her exam on the other, and in passing I expressed my puzzlement about this.

Granting the truth of these qualifications, it is, nonetheless, questionable business for students to relate their "hard-luck stories" to their instructors. Whatever wisdom may dictate on that side of the matter, however, its conclusion on the other side seems clear. It is not right for an instructor to allow the unfortunate circumstances of a student's life to influence his assessment of that student's work. For those who may agree that giving unfortunate students special grading considerations is not right, while having the uncomfortable feeling that comes from not knowing *why* it is not right, let me say some things that I trust will make its wrongness clear.

First of all, whether the student's problem comes from having to hold down one or more jobs while taking college courses, or derives from a handicap under which some illness or accident has placed the student, in neither case do the circumstances have any relevant relationship to the grade which the instructor should assign. The key word here is "relevant." Since within the context of higher education grades are supposed to be earned, non-earning activities and circumstances such as illness are irrelevant to the grade the instructor should assign. Being ill, as sad as that truly is, by itself is logically little more relevant to the grade the instructor should assign than is the color of the student's clothing on the day of the final exam; nor any more relevant than the fact that the student's father happened to have taken nearly the same course twenty-five years ago and passed it with flying colors.

One should go further and strictly say that even the grade earning activities *per se*, such as hard work, are ultimately irrelevant, because the final grade should be determined by the student's *performance* on all his course assignments, and not just on his grade earning activities. It is *performing highly* and not merely *trying hard* which secures the good grade. (This is what we were at pains to explain in complaints 3 and 6.)

Reading this distinction may precipitate an interesting question in the reader's mind. If the relevant factor in getting good grades is performance, and if a necessary condition for performing well is spending a required amount of time studying, and if working at three part-time jobs prevents one from studying the required amount, then doesn't it follow that working at three part-time jobs *is* relevant to getting good grades?

We can begin answering this question by drawing a distinction between *transitive* and *intransitive* relationships. This is because, at first glance, "being relevant to" seems like a transitive relationship.

If Albert is older than Benny and Benny is older than Caleb, then Albert is older than Caleb. Albert's relationship to Caleb is a transitive relationship.

More generally stated, *older than* is a transitive relationship. That is, the relationship holds from the first term to the third term just as it does, and just whenever it does, between the first term and the second term as well as between the second term and the third term. Letting "r" stand for the relationship we may abbreviate the definition as follows: If A r C whenever A r B and B r C, then r is a transitive relationship.

Whereas *older than* is a transitive relationship, *mother of* is not. It is an intransitive relationship. If Alice is the mother of Betty and Betty is the mother of Cathy then it does not follow that Alice is the mother of Cathy. Briefly, it is not the case that whenever A r B and B r C then A r C. The reader can exercise his imagination by trying to think of other intransitive relationships, such as *cousin of, friend of, taught by, influenced by,* etc.

It is important to notice in the above definitions that "r" retains the same sense when it is used between each of the three sets of terms, whether the relationship is transitive or intransitive. This fact will figure prominently in our analysis of the question above.

We can now approach the question directly. Abbreviated, it goes like this: "If outside work is relevant to study and if study is relevant to performance, and performance is relevant to getting good grades, then isn't outside work relevant to getting good grades?" The main problem with this question is that the word "relevant" is being used ambiguously. The word "relevant" is being used in a different sense in each of its first three occurrences in the abbreviated question.

1. Working at three part-time jobs is directly relevant to the business of studying, in the sense that the part-time work robs the student of the energy and time needed to study. The relevance here pertains to a direct causal relationship which working has on study: it directly reduces study time.

2. In the second use, the word "relevant" is not being used in the sense of "causes" but, instead, "contributes to." Studying is relevant to performance in the sense that it is one part, but only one part, of what is needed to get good grades. Performing well requires contributions from other sources as well, namely from academic ability and insight. Whereas outside work will directly cause the removal of study time and effective study, the act of effectively studying will not directly cause the good

performance that is needed to secure a good grade.

3. The word "relevant" takes on yet another sense as it is used in the third instance. A good performance is relevant to getting good grades in the sense that a good performance "warrants the getting of" good grades. Assuming that there has been no cheating, that the performance documents do not get burned up in a fire, etc., a good performance practically "guarantees the awarding of" a good grade. At least it "justifies the claim to be owed" a good grade. While we do not want to go as far as saying that a good performance is equivalent to a good grade, the relationship between the two is very close. Providing that the proper contextual conditions mentioned above have been met, one could say that a good performance is a sufficient condition for getting a good grade.

Given that the word "relevant" was used in three different senses in the foregoing question, there is not a transitive relevance relationship between working at three part-time jobs and getting a good grade. In fact, because of the ambiguity of "relevant" there is not a single relation here that is transitive, or not. Thus, we cannot say that working at three part-time jobs is relevant to the getting of good grades in the sense that performing well is relevant to the getting of good grades. But why should the third sense of "relevant" be the only sense that the instructor should employ when determining the grade of the working student, it may be asked.

There is a technique in logic which is used to establish the truth of a claim or a conclusion of an argument. It is called *reductio ad absurdum*. The claim or conclusion is shown to be true by first asking, what if it were *not* true? In other words, for the sake of exploring alternative possibilities, let us assume that the claim or conclusion is *not* true. If the claim is *not* true, the denial of the claim *is* true. If after assuming provisionally that the denial of the claim is true one discovers that accepting the denial lands one in an absurd position, one must accept that the denial cannot be true. If, therefore, the denial of the claim is absurd and thus untrue, then the claim must be true.

To summarize, one way of showing that a claim is true is, first, to deny the claim; second, to show that the denial is absurd; third, to infer that the claim must be true. For example, suppose that you want to show that the claim "I exist" is true. Assume provisionally that the denial, "I do not exist," is true. Since it is necessary for you to exist in order to make *any* assumption, you cannot successfully make an assumption which denies this obvious fact. Hence, if the denial "I do not exist" is absurd for you, and thus untrue, then the claim itself, "I exist," must be true.

We have said that the third sense of "relevant" is the only one that should be employed by the instructor when determining what grade to give the working student. Let us provisionally deny this and assume that more than just sense three of "relevant" may be employed by the instructor when assigning a grade to the working student. With nothing more to guide us, there seems to be no reason to restrict the number of senses of "relevant" to the range of senses found in one to three, or, to stop at any particular number of applications of one and two. Just as Paul's working at three part-time jobs is relevant to his meagre amount of studying, so his having three children is relevant to his working at three part-time jobs. And of course, being married to Sheril is relevant to his having three children. But he would likely never have met Sheril if the elevator where they first met had not stopped between floors for an hour, due to the carelessness of a service man working on an electrical cable near the shaft. Therefore, perhaps we should say that the service man's work was relevant to Paul's getting a poor grade on his test. Maybe Paul should blame *him* for the grade he got! Or, alternatively, if the suggestion is that a positive contribution has been made by the service man, because his work provided Paul with the excuse he needed to plead for more marks, then perhaps one could ask the registrar at Concordia to mail out a transcript to the service man with his name on it together with a passing grade on the course in which Paul was enrolled. Just think of the possibilities. Not only could students get good grades for merely studying the material, but they could rack up academic points by doing community service, and with a little ingenuity get a first class degree by successfully avoiding colleges classes altogether – with the exception of course of showing up for tests and exams to be able to demonstrate what little knowledge had been gained and therefore how much more deserving the attendance-challenged student really is.

We may say then that the third sense of "relevance" is the only one which is pertinent to Paul's deserving a good grade because if we do not accept this the consequences are absurd. Perhaps now it is a little clearer why student protestations, such as "but I read the book three times and studied my head off for the exam," sincere as they might be, are irrelevant (sense three) to the grade which he or she should get.

There is another, more personal aspect to this problem which we shall discuss briefly in order to complete the picture of the Paul-like student who questions his instructor about why he didn't get a good grade. When I learned that Paul was working at three part-time jobs while also trying to carry a full course load and sleeping only four hours a night, I was surprised, to say the least. In fact I found it mildly exhausting just listening to his account. And I assured him that I didn't think that I could have done any better than he had done if I had had to work under his constraints. Then I asked him if he thought that he was expecting too much of himself by aiming at getting good grades while holding down three part-time jobs and at the same time discharging his family responsibilities. Might he consider reducing his course load. Furthermore, I suggested that if he wanted any help in understanding his work I would be glad to give it. (The problem here of course is that a student has to find time to do enough work to determine both what he understands and what he does not understand. In short, learning about one's limits itself takes time – and this is just what Paul's work schedule did not allow him to do.)

Most of the instructors whom I know would also have been sympathetic with Paul's plight. And they, too, would have offered to help him understand his work. All of this they can do, and more. But what they cannot do, or at least should not do, is to substitute sympathy for performance, because performance alone can justly secure a good grade for the student.

In concluding this discussion, it might be mentioned that some instructors make allowances for a student's less-than-optimal performances on a final exam. They may give the student slightly more than he has strictly earned on the final exam. This may be due to the consistently superior work which the student has done over the year, or the outstanding class contributions which he has made, or both together. If, for example, a superior student needs a point or two to make a first class grade, many instructors will make up the deficit and award the first class grade. It is important to notice, however, that ultimately the gift is given on the basis of the student's performance. The deficit has been removed on the basis of what the student *has* done, and not on the basis of what he has *not* done; moreover, it is on the basis of work that is "relevant" to his performance, in the third sense of that term. The generosity is shown on the basis of *actual* past performance and not on the basis of an *imagined* past performance which might have been realized if only there had been time to do so.

12. "English is not my first language."

A student whom we shall call Broken paid me a visit during office hours. He was discouraged because he thought that he should have received a higher grade on his first philosophy test. Broken's mother tongue was not English and this undoubtedly had a significant bearing upon his dismal performance. *He* knew it and *I* knew it; but what each of us made of it was entirely different. Let us say that the language which Broken spoke was Foreignish. After explaining to Broken where he went wrong he said essentially this to me: "I'd like to see you try to learn Foreignish in the same period of time as I have tried to learn English and then I'd like to see you try to pass a philosophy test in Foreignish."

As I often do at the beginning of a course, I had in this case explained to the class of which Broken was a member, that the precise use of English is very important in the discipline of philosophy. Among other things, I said that the sentence "All elephants are grey" has exactly the same words in it as the sentence "Elephants are all grey," although the two sentences can and often do have different meanings. But not only is the precise placement of words important in structuring one's thoughts, I said, but so also is the coherence of ideas in a sentence. Incoherence can be created either by using grammatically incorrect sentences, or by using grammatically correct sentences containing ideas that clash. An example of the former is taken from an essay on censorship and free speech: "The option of change prior to or after the hurt may have occurred through speech is 'freedom.'" An example of the latter is taken from an essay on sexuality: "Men and women are basically the same in fundamentally different ways according to their kind." There is nothing grammatically wrong with that sentence, but you will do much better than I if you can get the ideas of the sentence to fit into a complete and coherent thought.

Despite my explanations to the class about the importance of the precise use of English, and even though I had reminded Broken of my previous remarks, he still seemed to think that the learning of English was a secondary matter and that I should make allowances for his incoherent writing. It was as though all my talk of the importance of precise expression had gone right over his head. It simply did not seem to register, for he was quite indignant that I should make so much of this business about the correlation between correct English and precise thought. Somehow, to his way of thinking, correct English was a nice but unnecessary feature of a good essay, an extravagant addition about which an instructor ought not to get too excited; for after all, the course *was* a philosophy course.

In one sense the attitudes of Broken and Paul were directly opposite from one another. Although working at three part-time jobs is not relevant to the awarding of good grades, Paul thought it should be. And although writing correct English is relevant to the awarding of good grades, Broken thought it should not be. Fortunately, something that Broken said during our conversation left me an opening through which to sail my main ideas.

At one point he seemed to be trying to convince me that he was very bright, that he had done well in mathematics, and that this fact should somehow make up for any weaknesses which may have been exposed on his test. I used this opportunity to point out that mathematics had standards of good performance and a language of its own which had to be learned before those standards could successfully be met, no less than philosophy did. One could imagine the reception that a student of mathematics would get from his math instructor if he were to use reasoning which was comparable to Broken's reasoning when complaining about the low mark he received on his calculus test. Suppose that he were to say something like the following: "Just because my multiplication and division aren't what they should be, and just because I don't know the rules for differentiation and integration, that doesn't mean that I deserve such a low mark on my test. You see, I didn't learn the basic operations of mathematics when I was in elementary and secondary school. Why are you judging me by the same standards as the ones you use to judge those who have learned the operations very well. I just don't 'speak' mathematics as well as the other students, and I haven't had as good an opportunity to learn." It is not hard to imagine what sort of reception such a line of reasoning might receive. I expect that the first response from the math instructor might well be one of mild paralysis – this comes from that peculiar kind of academic shock to which instructors are privileged. What precipitates the shock is the realization that even the most obvious conclusions will escape some people's notice. The point, to put it in a capsule, is simply this. It is the student's responsibility to meet the standards generally set by the discipline and specifically set by the instructor in the course which makes up part of the discipline. It is not the instructor's responsibility to waive the meeting of those standards or permit extraneous considerations to substitute for the meeting of these standards, in order to enable the disadvantaged or otherwise deficient students to do well and feel better about themselves. The course is there to be taken; it has standards which the student must meet if he wishes to succeed; he should not hope to succeed in the course by not meeting those standards. And since it is the students who are taking the course, and not vice versa, the old injunction applies: "Take it or leave it."[8]

Here again we need to conclude on a personal note, for the personal aspect is rarely absent in this sort of encounter between an instructor and a student. When Broken challenged me by saying that I would not likely be able to pass a test in Foreignish if I had studied it the same amount of time as he had studied English, I admitted as much, and said "precisely." And just as I would not pass in his language so it seemed that he might not pass in my language, given the same time constraints. And if neither of us would pass, it would be for the same reason. Neither of us would have met the standards required by the discipline. I commiserated with Broken and said honestly how well I thought he had done, given the short time during which he had been exposed to English. But unfortunately I also had to say that his progress, while admirable, might not qualify him to meet the passing standard of the course. I offered to give him some extra help if he chose to stay in the course; but he elected, wisely I think, to withdraw from the course.

5

Emotional Complaints and Disruptive Behavior

13. "This is a bunch of crap!"

On the very first day of classes I could tell that John would be a talkative student. Even while I was explaining the requirements of the course he wanted to get into an extended discussion about matters that seemed to be troubling him. The course was titled "Introduction to Western Philosophy." It took two semesters to complete, and it dealt with some of the most important classic texts in the history of philosophy. At the beginning I was therefore much encouraged at the prospect of having a student who would not be reluctant to start class discussions about the challenging material we were going to encounter over the next twenty-six weeks. It was not long, however, before my enthusiasm for his talkativeness waned. What seemed at first to be a student who would eagerly help me to create an intellectual ferment in the class turned out to be a student who created a climate of chaos.

As I learned much too late, John was a student who needed – no, demanded – the instructor's attention practically all the time. During some of my lectures I could barely speak three sentences before his hand would shoot up and he would ask a question or make a comment. Like so many other situations in life, this one was not simple. I wish I could say that all of John's questions and comments were irrelevant or obtuse and that I was able to subdue him by showing him repeatedly that his comments were off topic. But that would be untrue. Many of his comments were insightful and some were challenging, though it is also true that he had a tendency to wander from the material at hand. Still, one of the main problems was that John seemed oblivious to my verbal cues. I would say something like, "thank you for being willing to make a contribution, but I would really like to hear from other members of the class"; or, by addressing the other members of the class I would say, "don't let John have all the fun: what do some of the rest of you think?" Unfortunately, none of this seemed to register with John, so immediately his hand would go up again or he would just shout out a comment.

If his irrepressibility had been the only irksome trait with which I had to contend, his behavior might have been tolerable, though I am

65

certainly not advocating that one should tolerate a student persistently monopolizing class discussions. In addition, though, he would become visibly frustrated if he could not comprehend a passage that I was explaining or if he did not see the immediate practical relevance of what we were discussing. The result was that he became agitated and vulgar in class. One of the things he would say was, "this is a bunch of crap!" I, in my wisdom, would then adopt the role of a Socratic facilitator, and I would say, "John, *why* do you think that this is a bunch of crap?" This was supposed to create deep reflective impulses in John's psyche, from which he would eventually realize, by answering my questions, that what he had said was not only rash but out of place. But the reflective insight never materialized. John now had an audience; his claims became more exaggerated and were made with even greater conviction. Not wanting to betray confidence in my ancient mentor, I pursued the enlightenment of John with fervent questioning. I invited him to stay after class for a little talk. Sometimes a good analogy is worth a thousand words. So, I drew a parallel between the effluence which can pollute rivers and the vulgar speech which can pollute discussions. I informed him that I really could not allow anyone to use vulgar and abusive language when we were discussing philosophical issues because this would pollute our class discussions. When I finished my speech there seemed to be a calm resignation in John's eyes, as though he had seen the light. We talked amiably after the session and I felt gratified to think that John's behavior would now change. I was overly optimistic. The calm that I experienced was just the calm before the storm.

The matter of John's disruptive speech came to a head about half-way through the course. I was explaining Descartes' third meditation. It needs to be mentioned that this is considered to be a difficult piece of philosophical writing by the best of scholars; but for freshmen who are new to philosophy it is nearly impenetrable. That is why I normally spend at least three lectures on this meditation. At about the mid-way point of my exposition I could see that John's face was becoming unusually red and that he was agitated about something. Thinking that it would be better for him to voice his concerns than to combust, I tried to engage him in a discussion of the material. It was then that he erupted: "this is a bunch of crap!" (The actual words he used were more explicit.)

Parenthetically, we might imagine someone objecting to this kind of censorship on the basis of the claim that he had overheard a professional philosopher use an expletive when chatting with a colleague in the hallway of the philosophy department. In this scenario the faculty member used the expletive to evaluate the very philosopher whose arguments John found to be so frustrating.

The fact that a professional philosopher might think to himself or say in private what John said with gusto in front of the class does not change the verdict. First, a manner of speech should not be adopted simply because a philosopher uses it. Second, and more important, in the scenario which we have imagined, the faculty member tried to keep his disparaging comment in private, where it belongs.

The problem of John's behavior had to be resolved. I finally gave him an ultimatum: desist or leave. The brain cloud which seemed to block his understanding of Descartes lifted quickly, and I was surprised at how swiftly he was able to bring the consequences of his actions into clear focus. Although John's disruptive behavior did stop abruptly, I cannot say that it stopped in a mature manner. He dealt with the problem by attending classes only occasionally after that, and when he did show up, he remained conspicuously quiet.

I also wish that I could say that I had dealt with the problem in a mature manner at a much earlier time in the academic year, for there were a few unfortunate occurrences which resulted from my lack of perceptiveness. Before ever I confronted the problem in a suitable way, I received a prodding. A delegation of two students spoke to me after a class in which John had made one of his enthusiastic pronouncements about the value of the work we were studying. The first student to speak said that she was majoring in another discipline and that she was taking this philosophy course as an option. She was taking the course out of personal interest and liked the material we were studying. But she said that the class disruptions were preventing her from getting a deeper appreciation of the material that she thought was possible. Then she asked me an arresting question: "can't you see that by monopolizing the class discussions John is constantly drawing attention to himself?" It then hit me with considerable force that I had been cheating the rest of the class while trying to talk John out of his apparently intellectual problems. You might say that I was trying to solve a psychological problem with a philosophical solution.

On looking back I think that I was naive, although I ought to have known better. And it gives me no comfort to think that other academics might be afflicted with this same naivete, even those who teach philosophy. When I encountered John I was in what I shall call my "hyper-Socratic" period of teaching. I thought that any problem which arises in class could be solved with questions and answers. The clever instructor should be able to resolve any problem which he encounters just by using skillful word play. I probably wouldn't have admitted that much at the time, though I conducted my classes as though I believed it were true. To those who still believe it to be true, let me say a few more words on the subject.

The Socratic approach refers to a method according to which two participants engage in dialogue in order to discover philosophical truth. One participant asks questions and the other participant answers them. By a series of questions and answers the participants may presumably arrive at the truth about the matter which is puzzling them, such as the meaning of "justice." To be used successfully, this question-and-answer method requires that a number of conditions be fulfilled. The ones that most people hear about are those of the age and wisdom of the participants. The role of Socrates, the asker of questions, is played by the older and wiser participant; the role of the answerer of questions is played by the younger and less wise participant. The one who plays Socrates is supposed to be able to extract philosophical truth from the answerer by asking him clever and leading questions.

There are at least two other conditions which must be satisfied if this type of dialogical exchange is going to bear fruit. And these are not spoken of much in the academic community. The answerer must be *willing* to answer the questions – indeed, he should be eager to do so, for he, as much as the Socratic figure, should want to find the answer to the question which they find mutually puzzling. The second condition may be seen as a corollary of the first.

The answerer must have as his motive for willingly answering the questions the sincere desire to discover the truth about the matter which he and the questioner together are investigating. The second condition is especially important because certain kinds of insincere motives, followed by their corresponding actions, can easily send the whole process off the rails. And in my opinion, all the skill in asking questions which one could ever hope to possess will not enable the questioner to keep it on the rails if the answerer determines to undermine his efforts. A sincere willingness to answer the questions is crucial to the success of the Socratic method.

Occasionally you will find in one of Plato's dialogues a participant who becomes impatient with Socrates.[1] But the rude outburst is short-lived. It might seem from the dialogue that the participant's rudeness is suppressed merely by Socrates' clever response. That, I think, would be a superficial reading of the text. It would also be too simple an interpretation of what would actually be happening if the dialogue occurred in real life. A careful reading will reveal that the occasionally rude participants do not persist in their attempts to undermine Socrates' efforts in reaching his goal. Their irrational outbursts are transitory, not primarily because Socrates subdues them with a clever retort, but because *their* ultimate goal and Socrates' ultimate goal are in agreement with one another. Both have deep convictions about the meaning of the term under discussion, for instance, the term "justice." And both participants in the dialogue, the answerer as well as the questioner, are serious about convincing their opponent of his lack of understanding of the true meaning of the term. Still, the predominating impulse in both participants is *to resolve the issue at hand* and to follow the argument wherever it leads them. You may say that their motivations are the same.

The moral of the story seems to be that an instructor can successfully use the Socratic method with a student only if the student has a sincere willingness to co-operate with his instructor in the dialogical method of discovery, and only if that willingness is supported by enough self-control and discipline to permit the dialogue to proceed. It now seems to me wrong-headed to assume that an instructor should always be able to succeed in using the Socratic method, if only he is clever enough, no matter what the student's background and character are like.

There are students who arrive in our college classrooms whose lives are deeply troubled. Several of my colleagues get the impression that the number of such students is increasing, and that likely it will continue to increase in the foreseeable future. This is my impression as well. Seeing certain types of students behave according to a particular pattern every week for three to six months does, after all, provide an instructor with some material upon which to make an informed, albeit limited, judgment. And with that I will venture a few observations.

Some of the students about whom I have been speaking have such a craving for attention and such a need for recognition that they find it extremely difficult to follow the necessary rules for civilized discussion in an academic classroom. Perhaps there was a time not so long ago when such rules could remain unspoken and be taken for granted by an instructor. Now he often has to make his expectations concerning classroom decorum explicit at the beginning of each term. I have in mind simple rules pertaining to such matters as: raising your hand to be recognized before expressing your view; not interrupting someone while he is speaking, or, at least not doing so repeatedly; refraining from character assassination; rejecting the use of angry outbursts of emotion when the weakness of your position is being exposed, or when you are trying to get the upper hand in an argument; not monopolizing the discussions; etc.

We need to consider this situation carefully. Students who lack self-control and discipline perhaps have known 18-40 years of neglect, insecurity, low self-esteem, distrust of authority figures, and possibly physical and sexual abuse. Likely most of them will not have known all of these problems, though possibly most will have experienced some of them. The fact that they have gathered up enough courage to enroll in a university course is itself laudable. However, an empathetic diagnosis will not solve the problem to which I am here referring. Unfortunately, many of these students appear to have no personal acquaintance with the discipline, the commitment, the sincerity of intention, and simply the good manners which are required for a person to be highly successful in the academic world. I am not saying that they have never heard of these requirements; I am saying that the traits which naturally incline someone to meet consistently those requirements have not been inculcated into their characters – and they urgently need them. It would be rash to say that this deficiency can never be overcome, even by a determined 30 year-old who commits himself to making what will have to be a radical readjustment in his approach to dealing with people and solving problems. But it is not rash to say that such students labor under great handicaps, and that many of them will decide that the price of success in this personal area of work is too costly.

Unproductive mental attitudes and counter-productive emotional responses have been established and reinforced over many years. The idea that an instructor can always undo these self-defeating attitudes and responses, if only he is clever enough to find the right words each time he engages a student in discussion, is unrealistic. Do we really think that we can transform every undisciplined student in the classroom into a disciplined fair-minded inquirer with just the use of patience and clever repartee? How presumptuous!

At this point I need to face a direct challenge to my argument. Someone can easily say that in spite of my patience and willingness to help John out of his rut, in the final analysis I did not use the right classroom strategy with him. Put simply, I was not informed enough or clever enough, or both, to draw him out of his pattern of counter-productive responses. For if I had been equipped well enough, then his behavior would have ceased to be disruptive.

The assumption which lies behind this line of argument is that an instructor should be able to resolve any classroom problem like the one I have been discussing just by using questions and answers, because such a problem always can be resolved by using this method. Someone who is committed to this assumption, as I believe many people in the teaching profession are committed, might seem to have the basis for a strong argument. Because no matter how much evidence is presented for the claim that not all such problems are resolvable by using just the Socratic method, one can always say that in the cases put forth the instructors did not use the method skillfully enough. In brief, they must have left something out or misused the method. And if you were to ask why anyone would assume that some deficiency exists in the instructors' cleverness or in their skills in applying the method, the answer would be this: because all such problems can be resolved by using this method. Perhaps the reader can see already that the strength of this critical argument is only apparent. It takes on the appearance of strength by using chronic circular reasoning. If the support for the unconditional acceptance of the Socratic approach is achieved by persistently circling round to the assumption that the approach can always be successfully used, then the argument becomes chronically circular. In other words the argument appears to succeed by *begging the question.*

Imagine that I say to the believer in the unqualified potential of the Socratic method that such a method will not work with everyone, for instance, with John. The believer will then argue that I was not clever enough to employ the method effectively in John's case. What if I were then to present as further evidence for my position what actually happened, namely, that other instructors also tried unsuccessfully to help John function co-operatively in class using the Socratic method? The committed believer in the method would then say that these other instructors also lacked the necessary skills to help John. And if we were then to ask, "but why, in the face of such evidence, do you say that?," the believer in the method would say, "because one can deal successfully with any college classroom problem using the Socratic method, if only he is capable and experienced enough to do so." The believer in the method will not let anything falsify his position. However, to protect his position from falsification, he must resort to question begging, that is, to assuming the truth of the conclusion which he is required to establish; and again, he uses the conclusion which he is supposed to be establishing as the basic premise upon which he is trying to establish that very conclusion. When the premise and conclusion are repeatedly the same, you can assume that something is wrong.

My evidence is that there are some students in our colleges and universities whose lack of certain basic character traits makes it impossible for an instructor to guide them successfully in classroom discussions using the Socratic method. However, none of what I have said precludes the possibility of a instructor successfully using the Socratic method in class if a few of his students are *occasionally* bad-tempered, or even vulgar, for that matter. Though it should be stressed that in recognizing the need for a realistic margin of error in dealing with students I am not thereby condoning uncooperative behavior in the classroom, and certainly not encouraging it. Undesirable emotional outbursts and petulant behavior must be infrequent and transitory if a climate of cooperation is to be maintained. And such a climate is essential if mutual dialogical discovery is to take place. It might seem to someone who is unfamiliar with college teaching that because there are proportionately few students like John, the problem of classroom decorum is not a significant matter. That is not what I hear from my colleagues, either in the colleges or universities. I am always surprised at how much interest is generated among instructors when the topic of classroom decorum comes up. We shall see more clearly why this is so in just a moment.

The idea that an instructor must encounter someone like John before he can be said to have a significant classroom concern lacks a perspective which one gets from professional teaching experience. Imagine that you are standing in front of a class of thirty or more students between the ages of eighteen and sixty, and you are trying to communicate a long abstract message to them. If you are striving to be a good instructor you will be attempting to accomplish several goals almost at once. Some of your main goals will be as follows: to parcel out the message in a sequential, graduated fashion, that is, to make it systematic; to speak loudly enough for everyone to hear; to keep eye contact with students in the four quadrants of the room; to modulate your voice; to speak from different locations in the room; to answer questions; to engage the students in dialogue; to inject humor into your lecture at key points; and to ensure that you cover your material in the fifty minutes allotted to you. To accomplish all of these goals, or even to attempt to do so, takes concentration and energy; in fact often it is enervating.

Under such circumstances it does not take very many students to put you off stride. Two bundles of hopping hormones at the back of the class, whispering and making kissy faces at each another, may be quite enough to do it. In almost every class I have ever taught there has been at least one student of whom it might be said that he was vaccinated with a phonograph needle. The main complaint that I hear from instructors is that some of their students want to talk incessantly, and that by talking out of turn, they make it virtually impossible for the instructors to conduct their classes effectively. And it only takes one or two of such students in a class of thirty to create a distraction for several people. Students who want to talk all the time don't seem to realize, or, if they do realize, don't seem to care, that when they chat with their friends across the aisle it is distracting and annoying, not just to their instructor but also to their classmates who happen to be within hearing and viewing distance. Those who are distracted can easily number six or more. In the simplest terms, it is unfair to a class to permit a chatterbox to run unchecked.

A student does not have to be as impervious as John not to pick up social cues or even not to get a direct message delivered by his instructor. Some of these talkers will not get the message unless it is spelled out for them in no uncertain terms, together with attendant possible consequences for not heeding it. For the past seven years I have been using this approach in the first lecture of each introductory philosophy course that I teach. In my preface I stress the fact that I like lots of talking in my classes, and that I will positively prod students to participate in class discussions. Then I qualify my remarks by stressing that their talking and class discussions must be orderly if we are to accomplish our goals. For this reason I adopt one basic rule which everyone must follow: "no talking when someone else is talking who should be talking." By asking students to explain the relevance of the last four words I encourage them to enter into a discussion of the rule for discussions itself.

To summarize, then, it is perfectly permissible for a student to use argumentation to criticize the content of the course work he is studying and to complain about it being hard to understand or irrelevant or otherwise unacceptable. But all of this can be done without vulgarity and irrational outbursts of emotion. Indeed, unless the student is committed to criticizing and complaining in a disciplined fashion, there is little by way of dialogical discussion that an instructor can do to help him out of his ignorance. Vulgar speech and emotional outbursts promote imprecision in thought as well as an undisciplined approach to academic work, and therefore yield little or no insight. They discourage pride in mastering verbal skills and undermine that sense of accomplishment which comes from completing intellectual tasks. Lacking self-control, the student who uses these devices in class drags the discussion from the university to the back alley where thinking gives way to grunting. It isn't cute; it isn't educative; and it doesn't promote harmony among human beings.

6

More Complaints About the Instructor

14a. "You expect too much of us."

A great many of the arguments used in daily life are directed against people, their character and status, instead of against their ideas and what they say. Sometimes the character of a person does have a bearing upon the truth of what she says, as for instance in a person's testimony in a court of law. A lawyer will sometimes question the veracity of a witness on the basis of the fact that she has been known to lie under oath before, and perhaps is thought to be an inveterate liar. However, when the character or status of the people have nothing to do with the truth of what they say, then the arguments against the person are irrelevant. In the study of informal logic this type of irrelevancy is called an *ad hominem* argument, an argument *against the man.* "Don't trust what he says because he's divorced," "His moral views are out of touch because he's a fundamentalist Christian," "What does she know about raising kids; she doesn't have any!" are but a few examples of *ad hominem* arguments.

Sometimes students direct their arguments against their instructors instead of against what their instructors say in their syllabi, essay assignment sheets, and explanations during office hours. "You expect too much of us," complained Sandra who was unhappy with the grade she received on her mid-term test. Another student, David, said to me, "You're too picky," after I explained to him why he received the grade he did on his essay. And yet a third one, whose name was George, who was a little more sensitive to his situation, upon hearing the explanations for the marks deducted on his test, said, "You're very critical."

One of the interesting things about these complaints is that they might be true. An instructor must be vigilant that he or she does not set assignments and examinations which are excessively demanding or downright undoable. It has been said often enough that instructors are prone to forget what it was like to be a freshman or even a senior in college. Apparently, they seem to lack an assignments file in their folder of student memories. This is where the pattern of comments from students on formal evaluation forms may help an instructor to gauge the difficulty of his or her assignments appropriately. I say "pattern" because isolated examples of discontent can be found in the formal evaluation reports of even the most popular instructors.

But is the general claim that an instructor is too hard on his students relevant to the specific complaint which a student has about the grade which she received on her assignment? It would be difficult to argue cogently that it has no relevance at all. More defensible would be the claim that it does not have an immediate relevance. Only if the stringency of his requirements were applied to Sandra, for example, in a discriminatory fashion could we claim that his being too demanding had immediate relevance to Sandra's getting a poor grade. Assuming, however, that the instructor holds the same high, even excessively high, standards for all members of his class, Sandra's complaint about her grade, which is based upon the alleged severity of the instructor's overall marking scheme, is not immediately relevant to the matter at hand. What is immediately relevant is that a satisfactory explanation should be given to the student for her unhappy performance, and given in accordance with the same standards which have been applied to all other class members' essays.

An instructor may want to modify his old standards to enable all class members to earn a good grade more easily. But he should not want to change Sandra's grade upon the basis of his projected new standards – unless of course he intends to change consistently *all* the grades according to the new standard. That is sometimes done in classes where the performance is uniformly poor and the instructor recognizes that even his best students who should have been able to perform well were unable to do so.

To summarize, then, an instructor may or may not be expecting too much of a student who receives a poor grade on her assignment. He cannot reasonably discover the answer in the isolated complaint of that unhappy student. And if by considering the performance of the entire class, he later concludes that he has been too demanding on this assignment, he can still be completely fair to the complaining student by not even considering a change in her grade. Indeed he ought not to do so unless he is also going to change the grades of the members of the entire class. He might well do this, but then again he might not, possibly preferring instead to redress the imbalance by adjusting the degree of difficulty of the remaining assignments. One reason for taking the second course of action would be to stretch his students intellectually, to make them strive harder and not take the course for granted.

14b. "You're too picky."

When David said "You're too picky" and George said "You're too critical," they may have meant something quite different from what Sandra meant when she said "You expect too much of us." Moreover, this difference in meaning may have been unknown to the two men. Whereas Sandra used the words "expect too much" to refer to the general difficulty of her assignment, David and George most likely were using "too picky" and "too critical" to refer to what they perceived to be my excessive concern with the precise use of language. It was not the overall standards of performance that they were concerned about, that is, the conceptual difficulty of identifying and addressing the main questions posed by the assignment, but rather my excessive concern for precision in assessing their completed assignment. What this boils down to in many cases is a failure to appreciate the fact that scrambled grammar and fractured syntax can easily make a passage in an essay indecipherable. The sample sentence used in case study no. 12 illustrates the difficulty: "The option of change prior to or after the hurt may have occurred through speech is 'freedom.'"

Incoherence is also frequently achieved when ideas in one segment of a sentence have not been made to follow from, or conceptually fit with, ideas in another segment of the sentence. Three years ago I gave a freshman class an assignment which involved them in reading the first six chapters of Bertrand Russell's book, *The Problems of Philosophy.* The students were required to answer the following question: "Are Russell's search for certainty and his findings the same as Descartes?" In a passage in which one student was apparently writing about Russell's theory of the uniformity of nature I found this sentence: "Even if there is a law now that has no exceptions and applies significantly to our case, we are experiences, as well as our own."

Often in cases like these, only when the student is asked to read aloud the passage from his essay which his instructor has found to be opaque, and to explain phrase-by-phrase what the passage means, does it dawn upon the student that what he has written does not make complete sense. Pickiness is needed. It is an integral part of university training.

I am here reminded of the distinction between accuracy and precision.[1] The metaphor of shooting an arrow at a target will help us see the difference. To be accurate in shooting, one must aim in the right direction, one must find the right target. To be precise in shooting, one must hit the bull's-eye or an area close to it. Accuracy, then, is aiming in the right direction; precision is hitting the spot one is aiming at. One can be precise without being accurate, and conversely, one can be accurate without being precise. An example of the first case would be the hunter who jubilantly shouts "I got him right between the eyes!" only to discover upon approaching his dead prey that his arrow is lodged in the forehead of his hunting partner. An example of the second case would be the hunter who clearly sees a deer, aims at it, but misses it by two meters. Consider how this metaphor can be applied to student essay writing.

It is a matter of primary importance for a student to answer the question he is asked in a manner which takes into consideration all aspects of the question. Many essays go astray at the preparation and planning stage as a result of a student answering a question which the assignment has not asked. It is important for a student to aim his research attention in the right direction. It is equally important for him to aim his writing in the right direction: to make it accurate by making it follow a constructed plan which addresses the question of the assignment using the results of his research.

Unfortunately, having an accurate plan or proper direction for his essay, as necessary as that is, is not sufficient to enable the student to do well on his essay. He also requires the skill to put the details of what he wants to write in proper order. He needs precision in his writing as well as accuracy. Without precision, his message will be bent out of its proper shape and consequently he will not be able to successfully establish his thesis. Often this happens when generalizations are made, the imprecision resulting from the omission of one little word. The statement that "murderers, when they murder, cannot control themselves" is not a plausible claim. It can, however, be made plausible by placing one little word at the beginning of the sentence, the word "some." A student who writes the former statement may even have intended the latter. But his instructor, whose job is to read essays and not minds, will have to mark what he finds written.

A close inspection of the distinction between accuracy and precision as it applies to student essay writing reveals how precision directly affects accuracy. If a student misses the bull's-eye in enough sentences when he is developing a sub-thesis, he can miss the target of the sub-thesis altogether. It may be accomplished with only one sentence. And although one scrambled sentence will not cause the reader to miss the target of the entire thesis, three or more such sentences per page may be quite enough to do the job. I have read a few such essays which have succeeded in completely clouding the main thesis. Precision is so important to good writing that its absence adversely affects the accuracy of what an author is trying to say. It is difficult even to hit a target if one's skill in spotting and focussing upon the details of the target is lacking. Confucius once said: "If language is not correct then what is said is not what is meant, and if what is said is not what is meant, then what ought to be done remains undone."

13. "You don't like me."

Una's first language was not English and she had not been in the country more than ten years. She failed her first test in social ethics, though not by much. Seeing that her poor performance was in large measure due to her lack of language skills, I wrote a note at the end of her paper inviting her to visit my office to talk about her results. Soon after she arrived at my office she was in tears. She said, "I've been thinking that maybe you don't like Alienite students." This came as a mild shock to me because I thought I had made a deliberate effort at the first class meeting to make all students who were not fluent in English, including Alienite students, feel welcome. It is not easy to know what to say in a situation like this. A French expression comes to mind: "s'excuser, s'accuser," which applies to the written as well as the spoken word. Indeed it may be appropriate not to say anything, at least as far as the personal comment is concerned, and to address the identified shortcomings of the the test directly. Before doing this one can naturally ask a few exploratory questions such as, "why do you think that I don't like you?" The dilemma that an instructor faces in such a situation will become clearer as we examine this complaint in more detail.

All people, including students, can sincerely but mistakenly impute thoughts, attitudes and feelings to others. I suppose that all of us at one time or another have mistakenly thought that someone else was against us for some reason. We thought we saw displeasure in someone's eyes when in fact none was there, or we interpreted what he said in an unjustifiably dim light. I expect that many of us have had the experience of saying "good morning" to someone who did not say "good morning" back. And we thought for awhile that they were snubbing us, only to discover soon afterwards that on that morning the person was preoccupied with something. Perhaps it was an idea the person was developing; perhaps a quarrel he had just had with his spouse; or possibly it was bad news from his physician about the results of a blood test. Similarly, the student who thinks that his instructor doesn't like him may be sincerely but mistakenly imputing a negative feeling to his instructor.

Unfortunately the situation can be much more complicated than this, and the complication arises from the human capacity for pretense. We can pretend that someone has hurt our feelings when in fact the hurt has been completely fabricated. Why do we do this; why do we sometimes feign being hurt, by someone else's supposedly dirty looks, by his allegedly unkind words or by other imagined slights? The answer is simply this: to gain sympathy, to have attention taken away from our own responsibility for our plight, and dumped upon someone else, in this case an instructor. By making a pretense of being hurt by an alleged slight, an emotional indebtedness can be created in the instructor. The pretender hopes that this will cause him to think that he must work hard at making the student feel wanted and respected. One of the ways in which he can make his "hurt" student feel wanted is to assure him that, despite his dismal performance, at the end of the course he will pass. After expressing her feelings of not being liked, Una asked me to tell her what her chances were of passing the course.

It is not easy to know when someone's emotional response is sincere and when it is insincere. But in the final analysis one must make a judgment based upon the evidence at hand. If there is nothing to account for the student feeling that he or she is being treated unfairly – indeed if there is evidence to the contrary – then the very least an instructor is entitled to do is to wonder about the sincerity of the student. Of course in neither case, whether the student is sincere or insincere, ought he to allow his discernment in this matter to affect his judgment when grading the student's future assignments.

There is another dimension to this complaint which, because of its serious implications, we need to address openly. Discrimination[2] in all its various forms exists in our age as in previous ones. We have only to open the daily newspaper or talk to friends to discover evidence that people from many different segments of society are treated unfairly by others. This unfairness, though, is not limited to one class of people or to one type of numerical grouping. Not only are members of minority groups treated unfairly by members of majority groups but the members of majority groups are treated unfairly by members of minority groups. The former kind of unfairness gets lots of attention, the latter kind, none at all, at least as I see it. The reason is that we take too limited a view of the source of discrimination.

We have much evidence on the world scene to establish the belief that discrimination knows no bounds. It is part of the human condition. We can find discrimination of a serious kind in every country and in every group. It is found not merely between social groups but also within such groups. And it matters not whether the group you are looking at is black or white or red or brown or yellow or purple. In every group you will find unfair business practices, class pecking orders, and, generally, forms of snobbery and elitism whose outworkings exhibit an unfair treatment of some human beings by other human beings.

Again we do not hear very much about the fact that human beings, generally speaking, are discriminatory in their dealings with other human beings. It is much easier to find the source of the discrimination in a group, a class, or a color. It is much harder and certainly less comforting to deal with the view that people all over the globe have a mean streak in them, or whatever you wish to call that self-centred, socially destructive part of human nature.

Although the evil side of human nature is getting very little press these days, the evils of a certain political affiliation, a particular gender, a certain race or color are receiving enormous coverage. In fact, I think it fair to say that at this time the media in general are virtually seething with accounts of group-specific discrimination. It's in the popular ideological air that we breathe.

As a consequence, it is very easy for an allegedly disadvantaged group to gain sympathy by saying that the cause of their plight is the discriminatory behavior of another supposedly advantaged group. What the complaining group says might be true – but there is nothing in logic or in human nature which says that it must be true. Unfortunately, we have nearly come to the place where tabloid thinking governs our attitudes and behavior in such matters. The "underdog" is always right. Complaints are always substantial. For why would anyone complain about his or her condition if there were nothing to complain about? Since we do not put much stock in the belief that there is a dark side to human nature, a mendacious and socially destructive side, then we must turn to external forces for our answer. The answer, then, must be outside us, over there: in that group's practices, in that system's unfair rules, in society's institutions. In the fires of social indignation personal responsibility is consumed.

I have been writing about the climate of easy belief in our society which can make us too gullible when we hear complaints. But nothing that I have said implies that there are not legitimate complaints in our society and in our institutions. There are, and they ought to be addressed. We can see many forms of discrimination in our society, and where there is clear evidence that they exist we need to respond to them in the appropriate manner. We ought not to condone them; indeed we ought to condemn them.

But not every negative judgment which a majority member makes of a minority member or which a group of one color makes of a group of another color, should be called discriminatory. Possibly most of them are not. However, in our current climate of belief, where strong psychological associations have been established between certain groups and justified complaining, the real danger exists that such groups will trade upon established sympathies by complaining insincerely and/or mistakenly. A further consequence of this climate of belief is that in some cases people who are in positions to make accurate diagnoses of certain social problems are afraid to do so because they fear that they will be charged with some form of discrimination. Not daring to pinpoint the problem, they skirt it. A social problem which is not addressed becomes not just a problem which is not solved, but also a problem which is magnified.

Terms of severe judgment are used to censor socially undesirable behavior or ideological views. Sometimes the terms are justly applied; sometimes they are unjustly applied. In the political sphere, if someone wishes to dismiss the views of a candidate or party he may say "oh, he's a socialist," or "she's a right-wing tory," or "he's a radical reformer," etc. These terms have both a negative and positive connotation, depending upon who is using the terms and who is listening to them. But it is easy to censor someone who holds a view just by speaking the terms of identification in a voice with a certain inflection. Can't you hear it: "oh, no wonder he believes in centralizing the services, he's a socialist!" as though just saying the word "socialist" in a certain way is enough to establish the falsity of the views of the person of that persuasion.

The same easy dismissal occurs in the religious sphere. In order to cast aspersions upon the views of a certain religious person it is quite enough to call him a "fundamentalist." Although this word also has both a positive and negative connotation, depending upon who is voicing it and who is listening to, I surmise that those for whom it has negative connotations far outnumber the ones for whom it has a positive connotation. And again, it is easy to hear in one's imagination the inflection which casts a negative evaluation upon the person who is being criticized.

To the question, "was there any opposition to the rally?" one might well hear the response, "no, just a bunch of fundamentalists carrying placards." By just saying the word "fundamentalist" in a disdainful manner people try to dismiss out of hand what the religious person of that persuasion believes. And many who do this are successful, because this kind of illogical thinking resonates with the thinking of many others. When the others hear someone utter a term which captures their own unexamined prejudices, it makes them feel comfortably correct.

Perhaps the most abusive term of censorship is the term "racist," although here, too, there are a few people who apply the term positively to themselves. Most of us are grateful that their numbers are proportionately few. It is such a potent term because the people to whom it may properly be applied say and do things which have horribly dehumanizing consequences.

Philip W. Cummings has defined racism as "the doctrine that one group of men is morally or mentally superior to another and that this superiority arises out of inherited biological differences." What makes it such an odious doctrine is that "the tenets of racism . . . lead to moral conclusions that contradict many of the most generally accepted civilized standards and have notoriously led to what on ordinary grounds are inconceivable crimes." Cummings also argues that ". . . the tenets of racism are not merely unsubstantiated by the facts but in large measure contradicted by the facts."[3] Therefore the racist believes not only in the superiority of one race and the inferiority of the others, but also believes that in virtue of this alleged superiority, the "superior" race may treat the "inferior" races in a manner which would only be called unfair or murderous if the treatment were exhibited between members of the supposedly superior race. Because racism breeds a virulent strain of unjustified hatred, we ought to reserve the word "racist" for the qualified recipients of it. To take it upon our lips is a serious matter. I'm afraid, however, that the term itself is being misused in our society and the consequences of its misuse are deplorable.

I tell my students that terms of severe judgment can be used as labels. We slap them on the foreheads of people whom we want to censor. The label may in some cases fit the person on whom we slap it; but even then, too often by using this labelling act we divest ourselves of the responsibility of thinking. Instead of addressing a problem analytically and trying to find a solution, we can too easily just label it. But worse than that, we can slap a label on a person to whom it *does not* fit, and the results are sometimes disastrous. Even an acknowledgement of wrong doing, of having misapplied the label, unfortunately does not undo the damage which has already been done. Too often when you try to remove a label, you are not successful. You get some of the paper off, but the glue sticks. Retractions, apologies and even legal vindication do not remove the suspicion which sticks in the minds of many people who first heard and chose to believe the charge. It can easily ruin someone's career. Perhaps a person who glibly or otherwise insincerely labels someone a "racist" ought to be dealt with severely and made a spectacle of. He ought not to be permitted to slink into anonymity while the target of his false accusation in full public view struggles to live with a besmirched reputation.

Certainly there is racism in our society; where there is clear evidence that it exists, we ought to fight it with determination. But most criticisms by members of one race, of members of another race, should not be called "racism." Unfortunately, those who trade upon the superficial observation that a criticism has been made across racial boundaries do themselves, their race and the human community itself a grave disservice. Examples can be multiplied.

Take for instance the supervisor of one race who justly criticizes his subordinate who happens to be of another race for any one of a large number of unacceptable behaviors in the work place: being chronically late, spreading rumors in the unit, slacking off, repeatedly taking unauthorized or over-extended breaks, making unauthorized use of company tools for personal gain, and the list goes on. Suppose that the subordinate cries "foul," that he complains to the higher administration that his supervisor is discriminating against him because he belongs to a different race. This is how someone can trade upon a superficial racial difference in order to mask a deep problem or personal irresponsibility. More troubling still is the distinct possibility that the supervisor will not have confronted his irresponsible subordinate in the first place. Anticipating that the subordinate will cry "foul" and wanting to avoid the stress which inevitably comes from dealing with such false accusations, he avoids confronting his subordinate about his unacceptable behavior. In fact he skirts the main problem. He may for instance present a proposal to his own supervisor for the hiring of more people in his unit. This will nicely take up the slack created by his irresponsible subordinate. But the problem will not go away; rather, it will likely become magnified. This is because the supervisor's evasive action will send a clear message to the irresponsible subordinate that he can get away with shoddy behavior in the workplace. Nor does the magnification stop there; for this subordinate's behavior will not go unnoticed by other workers in the same unit. It will not take long before they too will start robbing the company of working time or something else because they will have seen in their fellow subordinate a living model of the idea that there is no penalty for shirking one's responsibility in the work place.

We have travelled a fair distance from the seemingly innocuous account of the student who thought her instructor did not like her, to a discussion of the manipulation of an instructor by negative innuendo, to an account of the insidious labelling of people through the use of terms like "racist." Just as in the case of appealing grades, so in this case as well, if there is clear evidence that an instructor is discriminating against a student, then it ought to be presented to the academic administration responsible for handling such complaints. As there is usually a procedure set up in most institutions for dealing with appealed grades, so there is usually some procedure which can be invoked for dealing with complaints about unjust discrimination.

But what about the insincere complaint, the one which is made knowingly without evidence? What should be done about a student who without any supporting evidence suggests in a soft voice that her instructor is giving her a low grade because he dislikes the group to which she belongs? The only support which can be called on her behalf, being no support at all, is her poor academic performance. Are there any procedures in place for dealing with such insincerity among students, and should there be?

This might be thought to be a trifling matter in light of the overall duties which an instructor has, and to which he ought to give no more attention and thought than the detailed explanation he provides to the complaining student for the comments he has placed upon her failed test. Simply let it pass, in other words. This may be the right course of action; I'm not sure. I have a nagging doubt, however, that in letting it pass, an instructor will be sending a signal to students that they may say what they like without paying for it. Moreover, I cannot help thinking that if it were shown that an instructor was discriminatory in his grading practices it would not be considered a trifling matter, and the business of retribution most assuredly would not be overlooked.

Just as in the example above, where the supervisor overlooked the condemnable behavior of his subordinate, so in this case too, an instructor may let such implicatory remarks from a student pass in order not to draw attention to himself and, as they say, create more trouble than it is worth. But should he do this?

We might call ours the age of accountability. Everyone, including politicians, clergypersons, academic administrators, teachers at all levels, physicians, psychologists, among others, is being scrutinized and asked to give an account of the behavior which their clients consider unwelcome. Much coverage is given to these complaints by the media. The question for us here is: shouldn't students who complain have to give an account of their complaints too? And shouldn't complaints which are shown to be fabricated be dealt with in a manner which will discourage students from fabricating more complaints? Perhaps the severity of the student's punishment should be indexed to the severity of the instructor's punishment in a case where the instructor is found to be guilty.

There is another interpretation of the complaint "you don't like me" which we need to look at before concluding this section. The implications of the truth or falsity of this interpretation are not as far reaching as those of the interpretation which we have just examined. I am referring to the common experience of meeting people every day whom we do not like. Someone may "rub us the wrong way"; his personality may be "too aggressive" or "too wimpish"; he may be "too loud" or "too quiet"; she might be "too silly" or "too serious"; perhaps she is too interested in money for our liking, or perhaps she is too much out of touch with daily commerce; she is too this or too that or too something else. If we face this issue frankly we shall have to admit that sometimes what seem to others to be insignificant details, seem to us to be annoying characteristics. Someone can become "turned off" by another person's "grating" voice, his "garish" clothing, her "self-centred" conversation, his "boorish" table manners, and so forth. It is amazing to see how such a large repulsion can be created by such a small mannerism. This is the way we are, and we need to face it.

But we dare not stop here. One of the signs of personal maturity is the ability to get along with people whom we do not like. And in the event that we meet someone with whom we just cannot get along, the least we should demand of ourselves is that we treat that person fairly. It is not too much to ask that instructors possess such maturity; nor should it be out of place to expect students to have the same. It is to be expected – in fact, practically guaranteed – that during a student's college career he will meet at least one instructor who, as far as he is concerned, is offputting. In brief, he won't like the instructor. But the comforting thing about this is that he needn't feel guilty at all for thinking this way. For chances are, the instructor won't like him either! Where is it written that we should be able to like everybody? Respect them? Yes. Treat them fairly? Most assuredly. Love them in the Biblical sense? Yes, that too. But like everybody? No, certainly not. Our emotions simply won't allow it.[4]

There is a trap to be avoided in arriving at this frank admission. It is the temptation to think that because we cannot like everybody we are justified in excusing ourselves for treating those whom we do not like in an unfair or unkind manner. The conclusion does not of course follow.

7

Counterpoint

There is another side to this story of groundless student complaints. Indeed, there are at least two other sides. And books have already been written about one of them.[1] I refer to the behavior of instructors who do not take their teaching responsibilities seriously and about whom students have a right to complain. Well documented are cases of instructors who show up late for classes, whose lectures are a jungle of ideas, whose aimless ramblings in class frustrate students who need help in understanding the course content, whose syllabi tell their students nearly nothing about what is expected of them, who don't keep office appointments, whose preoccupation with their own research makes them forget what *they* felt like as insecure freshmen on a large university campus, and so on. I once knew an instructor who wrote his lectures notes on the back of a cigarette package and delivered them with the ponderous solemnity of an undertaker substituting for a priest at a poor funeral.

Now, some professor reading this may be tempted to think that "such notes could contain an important formula like $e=mc^2$ or they might be simply the schematic outline of careful work done previously." It grieves me to report that Einstein was not at work in this case, nor had many hours of conscientious preparation preceded this instructor's doodling. Not even all the scribbling of a great mind is worth reading, and it's for certain that impromptu scribbling alone will not a great mind make. Even less will it make a great lecture.

Such irresponsible behavior, of which too many students have been the unfortunate recipients, sometimes stems from a jaded view that some instructors have of students and their place in the academic community. Instead of seeing them as sensitive human beings whose minds they can help to mold for the good of society, they see them as nuisances. I was once told of an instructor who said that "students are to a university what pigeons are to a cathedral." No doubt he loved his work. I guess he was so successful in keeping the holy place clean that no worshippers ever felt worthy to enter.

I can't pretend to be writing from a plateau of perfection in this business of giving students their due, and the reader may be assured that my own behavior in some areas of instruction has fallen short of the goal which everyone in the teaching profession should aspire to achieve. But one of the things that I have been at pains to convey in this book is that we do ourselves and our society no good by rationalizing away our own weaknesses and failures – whether we speak as instructors *or* students.

Another side to the story about which we have said nothing concerns those students whose authentic academic behavior is a joy to behold. In this regard I think first of Jean-Paul. He wasn't getting the grades he wanted on his essays, so he asked me why. Among the things that I said afflicted his essays was an unclarity of expression due to poor grammar and awkward syntax. In many places I simply didn't know what he was saying. He took this information home to mull it over, and being not entirely convinced by my explanations, decided to test the intelligibility of his writing on his wife, whose opinion he respected. Later he visited me in my office to report his wife's uncompromising judgment. After reading two of his essays she said to him, "You don't know what you're talking about!" I am not now appealing to Jean-Paul's wife to give support to my assessment of his essays. The point of the story is that Jean-Paul was ruthlessly honest with himself and with me. He didn't have to make a special trip to my office to tell me the results of his private experiment or of his coming to accept my earlier explanations. I thought it took strength of character for him to do that, and I told him so. Moreover, and sadly, I couldn't talk him out of dropping the course.

Ping is another student whose unblinkered judgments about her own academic performance is memorable. She stayed after class to ask for clarification of something I had said in my lecture and which her fellow students took up in the class discussion. Near the end of our conversation she volunteered that she enjoyed philosophy more that any of her other courses even though her lowest mark was in this subject. One of the things which signalled her sincerity in this admission was her further comment that she thought she didn't have the skills needed to earn the grade she wanted. She wasn't cleverly saying that because of her wonderful honesty she deserved special consideration. Not only what she said, but also how she said it, precluded that possibility. I gave her some suggestions which she applied conscientiously and as a result she raised her mark by about ten percent on the subsequent assignment.

And thus a book could have be written about the responsible students I have been privileged to know. But that is not the book I thought needed to be written at this time, and hence the reason for the emphasis which has been made in these pages.

If I were a prophet or seer I might be able to make some wide-ranging generalizations with confidence. Being neither, I have only impressions which derive from my teaching experience, from my knowledge of the experiences of others, and from personal observation and study. Those who read these words will have to say *yea* or *nay* in light of their own observation and experience. That notwithstanding, I am struck by the consistency of concern which I hear in the voices of numerous teachers at every level of the public and private systems of education.

As I see it, an unhealthy moral climate has settled upon the student world, but which by no means is found exclusively there. It is a climate whose main elements I surmise have been present wherever there have been instructors and students in a teaching-learning environment, yet whose influence seems to be stronger today than it was a few decades ago and whose strength seems to be building. This weather system has already been discussed in detail in the previous chapters and some of its main elements can be captured in statements of stereotypical thinking: "Someone else is responsible for my failure"; "People don't complain unless they have good reason to complain."

Political opinion today is such that if we talk about the irresponsible behavior of instructors, all ears snap smartly to attention and all human sensitivities align themselves indignantly against it. But public sentiment is not nearly so responsive when we talk about irresponsible student behavior. Anyone who addresses the issue is liable to encounter nervous opposition. The same goes for other "touchy" moral issues in our society, and for the same reason: they put commonly perceived victims in something less than a flattering light.

Many people today don't seem to know that humanity isn't neatly divided into *the good guys*, who have the big *G* on their T-shirts, and *the bad guys*, who have the big *B* on theirs, with the former group living at one end of town and the latter group living at the other. Specifically, such people are not keenly aware of the fact that *the bad guys* are within us, and that *we* are just as capable of being nasty as the other guys, and often we are. And being unaware of this aspect of our human nature – at least being unwilling to face it – they then neglect to teach this insight to their children. Hence the attitude "my failure is your responsibility."

The most excellent place to learn personal responsibility is in a loving and stable family where, among the other virtues, the making of discriminating moral judgments, including frank judgments about one's own behavior, is taught on a daily basis. Students desperately need this early training and our society won't survive very well without it.

Notes

1

[1] I do not claim to have exhausted all the possible interpretations of Jillian's and other students' concerns.

[2] Here "anti-religious" can be substituted for "non-religious" where the substitution describes the situation more accurately.

[3] As well, the topic may be a person or a group of people.

[4] For more on circular reasoning and question begging see complaint 13, p. 65f. Texts useful in the study of basic logic can be found in endnote 8 below.

[5] It does not improve the picture to say that the locution "he didn't like my essay" is merely an elliptical way of speaking, adopted by students to protect their self esteem, because they would never want to admit to their friends that they were, for example, incoherent on their essay. In this case the student's performance cannot be put in a better light unless the instructor's evaluation *is* cast in a darker one. More precise words like "incoherent" are replaced by less precise words like "didn't like" because, whereas logical and grammatical judgments have a large measure of objectivity to them, likes and dislikes do not. The more the instructor's evaluation can be viewed as subjective, the less seriously should his evaluation be taken to be; and of course the less deficient the student's work becomes.

[6] What the percentage of instructors is, who possess the spirit of generosity of which I have been speaking, I cannot say. Indeed it may even be doubtful that a questionnaire could be designed to guarantee an accurate answer to such a question. Of course the anecdotal evidence about instructors who are ungenerous is legion. But even supposing, for the sake of argument, that more than fifty percent were mean-spirited, this would not undermine the argument which I have been making about the possibility of critical openness. Though, granted, knowledge of such a statistic would almost certainly increase the anxiety of students.

[7] *The New Encyclopaedia Britannica,* 15th edition (Chicago: Encyclopaedia Britannica Inc., 1989) Vol. 4, p. 47.

[8] In all that has been said we have been assuming that the rules for constructing good arguments and avoiding bad ones can be understood and applied by students as well as instructors. It is granted, however, that students will usually have to be introduced to the rules and will have to practice using them for a considerable time before they feel as comfort-

able with argumentative analysis as their instructors. Stated simply, "an argument is a group of [statements] of which one, the conclusion, is claimed to follow from the others, which are its premisses." (Copi, p. 15) It is often at the level of the basic premiss of an argument that the most entrenched biases can be found. Students can develop the skill to recognize their own biases as well as those of their instructor through a study of the elements of good and bad argumentation. Such a study can usually be undertaken by enrolling in an informal or practical logic course at college or university. The student for whom the study of argumentation is brand new, and who does not wish to enroll in a basic logic course, can profit from reading on her own Anthony Weston's *A Rulebook for Arguments,* 2nd ed. (Hackett Publishing Co., 1993). For more thorough and comprehensive work in basic logic the student should consult Trudy Govier's *A Practical Study of Argument,* 3rd. ed. (Belmont, CA: Wadsworth Publishing Co., 1992), or Irving M. Copi & Carl Cohen's *Introduction to Logic,* 9th.ed. (Toronto: Maxwell Macmillan Canada, 1994).

[9]I haven't said anything in the main text about biases in the maths and sciences. One of the reasons for this is that I don't feel qualified to do so. Nevertheless, I am going to hazard a speculative comment here, in this more tentative region of the text. My observation is based upon my weak acquaintance with matters scientific and upon my strong acquaintance with professionals working in the area. I am told by one of my friends who is an instructor of mathematics at a nearby university that, despite popular opinion, there is a fair degree of subjectivity even in this reputedly most precise science. Unless a proof which a student submits to his instructor is utterly nonsensical, on the one hand, or breathtakingly elegant and original, on the other hand, there will be much room for subjective judgment so far as marks to be awarded are concerned. For instance, a judgment will have be made in the case of a student who doesn't have a completed proof but who gets part of the main idea; or, alternatively, gets the main idea but fails, for lack of time or lack of insight, to derive the right answer. Unless a right-or-wrong approach is taken with respect to the student's result, which is not, as is commonly thought, the usual approach, then the methodological biases or prejudices of the instructor are bound to enter. It seems to me, then, that although the biases and prejudices of a philosophy instructor are likely to be potentially more obtrusive than the biases and prejudices of a mathematics instructor, into the teaching and grading of the respective subject matter, the students of the math instructor to some degree will have to contend with biases as well. Therefore, perhaps it is not too much to say that what we have claimed about bias, prejudice and dogmatism with respect to liberal arts subjects applies to science subjects moderately well.

2

[1]And of course just as there are characteristics which make philosophy stand out from English as a university discipline, so there are characteristics which make English stand out from philosophy. What we are saying about philosophy we can in principle also say about English.

[2]This does not mean that the instructor should *never* take the comments which a student conveys from an outside authority seriously.

3

[1]"To a Louse," Russell Noyes, ed., *English Romantic Poetry and Prose* (New York: Oxford University Press, 1956), p. 158.

[2]James Rachaels, "Euthanasia," *Matters of Life and Death,* Tom Regan, ed., (New York: Random House, 2nd.ed., 1986), p. 39.

[3]If the textual material is easy enough to grasp without the aid of an instructor, and if the instructor does not use extra-textual material in his lectures, and if the size of the class makes asking questions and dialogical communication prohibitive or impossible, then of course the student might just as well save himself a drive to the university. However, if all these conditions are frequently satisfied in our institutions of higher learning, then we do have a scandal on our hands.

[4]Yes, it is possible for the faithfully attending student to sleep his way through even my classes. I never said my plan was perfect. I only mean to argue that for the vast majority of students it will be much better for them to attend university classes that to miss them. And attendance is what I want to encourage. By the way, I do also tell them that I will not phone them at 3:00 a.m. to ask them why they weren't in class the previous day. In fact I assure them that my aim in all of this is to reward those students who show up regularly for classes and help create an interesting learning environment for everyone present – and not to police their personal lives.

[5]Concordia uses a grading scale which measures from 1 to 9. In general terms, 4 is a pass; 5 is fair; 6 is good; 7 is very good; 8 is excellent; 9 is outstanding. Failing grades are found in the range of 1 to 3.

[6]For instance, perhaps the student had an aversion to the subject matter which made his hard work less productive than it could have been. These odd situations which come up from time to time, and whose importance I have no wish to minimize, do not constitute the complaints to which we have here limited our attention.

4

[1]The alternative title was suggested to me by Susan Dywer.

[2]I am grateful to John King-Farlow for this point.

[3]The action is unfair unless there is some reason to justify it, as in the case where a grade is close to a higher one and there is reason to give the higher grade. Perhaps then, we could say more precisely that it is unfair for a student to expect to receive a grade he did not earn. Though, if a student is bumped up to the next grade because of his performance in class it would be only fair to give other such deserving students the same nudge. The rule here is to give equal grades for work of equal value. Here is where a classmark can serve a useful purpose. It can be used as an instrument to adjudicate between a higher and lower grade.

[4]I have borrowed this quotation, or facsimile thereof, from some author whom I would very much like to acknowledge; but unfortunately I've forgotten the source.

[5]There are other possible reasons for our behavior, such as a lack of discipline. But even if this were the reason, the question would still remain as to why we should take pride in a lack of discipline, instead of bragging about its symptoms.

[6]A comprehensive book which students in high school and college have found helpful is David Ellis' *Becoming a Master Student,* 7th ed. (Boston: Houghton Mifflin Company, 1994). The subject matter covered in the book is mentioned in its sub-title: *Tools, techniques, hints, ideas, illustrations, examples, methods, procedures, processes, skills, resources, and suggestions for success.*

[7]To avoid any misunderstanding perhaps I ought to mention that naturally I kept my judgment to myself during our conversation, for obvious reasons.

[8]This says nothing against the possibility of adjusting the requirements of a course if they are perceived by an instructor on reflection to be too tough for the students to satisfy. But in this case certain basic academic standards are still preserved and everyone who takes the course is still required to meet them.

5

[1]See the early part of the *Republic* where Thasymachus enters the discussion with anger, frustration and sarcasm: Book I 336, 343.

6

[1]The distinction was suggested to me by Onora O'Neill's essay, "The Moral Perplexities of Famine and World Hunger," in Tom Regan, ed., *Matters of Life and Death*, 2nd ed., (New York: Random House, 1986), pp. 293-337. She applies the distinction to moral theories: "In practical affairs it is more important to find a theory whose recommendations reliably point in the right direction [i.e., one which is accurate] than it is to find one that will provide a finely detailed code of conduct [i.e., one which is precise]." (p.299)

[2]Discrimination in life is necessary, and many forms of it are good. That is, the word "discrimination" has a positive connotation as well as a negative one. In the discussion which follows in this case study, however, I shall be examining a bad form of discrimination, the kind of unfair discrimination which would take place if an instructor were to determine the grade of a student on some basis other than that of the performance standards by which all members of the class should be assessed. For ease of reading throughout the discussion let the word "discrimination" mean "unfair discrimination."

[3]"Racism," Paul Edwards, ed., *The Encyclopedia of Philosophy* (Collier Macmillan Publishers: London, 1967), Vol. 7, p. 58.

[4]Immanuel Kant argues that ". . . love out of inclination cannot be commanded; but kindness done from duty . . . is *practical* . . . love, residing in the will and not in the propensions of feeling. . . ." *Groundwork of the Metaphysics of Morals*, translated by H.J. Paton, (New York: Harper and Row, 1964), p. 67.

7

[1]E.g., *Saints and Scamps: Ethics in Academia* (Totowa, N.J.: Rowman and Littlefield, 1986, recently reissued by University Press of America) by Steven M. Cahn. In this wise little book Cahn provides his reader with examples of the following: professors who have behaved unethically (pp. 1, 2) and irresponsibly (p. 7); a professor who did not keep deadlines which he himself had set (p. 16); a professor who refused to learn the names of his students even though his class was small (p. 18); professors whose laziness and selfishness kept them from furnishing their students with the guidance they needed (p. 98); professors whose squabbling made it impossible for a Ph.D. student to finish his work (p. 99).

Printed in May 1996 by

in Boucherville, Quebec